CHATTING TO LEARN

CHATTING TO LEARN

The Changing Psychology and Evolving Pedagogy of Online Learning

James M. Hudson

CAMBRIA
PRESS

YOUNGSTOWN, NEW YORK

Library of Congress Cataloging-in-Publication Data

Hudson, James M.
    Chatting to learn : the changing psychology and evolving pedagogy of online learning / James M. Hudson.
        p. cm.
    Includes bibliographical references and index.
    ISBN 978-1-934043-72-1 (alk. paper)
    1. Internet in education. 2. Learning, Psychology of. 3. Instructional systems—Design. 4. Communication in small groups. I. Title.

    LB1028.43.H83 2007
    371.33'44678—dc22

2007019973

*To Vi and Luna, who keep me smiling
even on the cloudy days.
I love you both very much.*

TABLE OF CONTENTS

List of Figures   xii

List of Tables   xiii

Foreword   xv

Preface   xvii

Acknowledgments   xxi

Abbreviations   xxiv

Chapter 1: Chatrooms and Learning Behaviors   1
    1.1 The Challenge of Online Learning   1
    1.2 Research Questions   3
        1.2.1 Conversational Equity:
            A Case Study   5
        1.2.2 Discussion Quality: A Quasi-
            Experimental Study   6
    1.3 Looking Forward   7

**Chapter 2: Chatrooms and Small
            Group Learning**   11
    2.1 Chatrooms and Small Group Learning   11
    2.2 The Uniqueness of Text-Based Chat   12
        2.2.1 Linguistic Features of
            Chat Conversations   13

2.2.2 Behavioral Features of
Chat Conversations   15
2.2.2.1 Self-Awareness   16
2.3 Important Learning Behaviors   18
2.3.1 The Importance of Conversational
Equity   18
2.3.1.1 Social Status and Inhibition   20
2.3.1.2 An Interesting Domain:
Foreign Language Learning   23
2.3.2 The Importance of Perspective
Taking   28
2.3.2.1 An Interesting Domain:
Professional Ethics Education   31
2.4 Learning with Technology   33

Chapter 3: Explaining Equity: A Case Study   **37**
3.1 Questioning the Causes of Behavioral
Changes   37
3.2 Patterns of Participation in Foreign
Language Learning   39
3.2.1 Conversational Dynamics   40
3.2.1.1 Prof. Sagnier   44
3.2.1.2 Prof. Poulain   49
3.2.2 An Aside: New Social Expectations   50
3.3 Explaining Behavioral Changes   51
3.3.1 The Bystander Effect: A Lens
for Understanding Participation   53
3.3.2 Case Study: Participation in
IRC Français   58
3.4 Discussion   68
3.4.1 Learning   68

3.4.2 Self-Awareness 71
3.4.3 Social Cues 76
3.4.4 Blocking 77
3.4.5 Diffuse Responsibility 80
3.5 Alternative Interpretations 81
3.6 Summary 83

Chapter 4: Interaction Quality:
A Quasi-Experimental Study **85**
4.1 Studying "Quality" 85
4.1.1 Defining "Quality" 86
4.2 The Research Setting: CS 4001 89
4.2.1 The Role of Small Group
Discussions 92
4.2.2 A Typical Class Session 95
4.2.2.1 Arrival 96
4.2.2.2 Introductory Lecture 98
4.2.2.3 Small Group Discussion 99
4.2.2.4 Wrap-Up/Report Out 100
4.2.3 The Everyday Problems of
Participation in CS 4001 100
4.2.3.1 Too Little Time 101
4.2.3.2 Class Size 102
4.2.3.3 Motivation 102
4.2.4 Behavioral Changes in Online
Pilot Studies 103
4.3 Quasi-Experimental Method 105
4.3.1 Data Collected 105
4.3.2 Quantifying "Quality" 108
4.3.3 Developing a Standard of
Comparison 110

4.3.4 "Grading" the Discussions   114
4.3.5 Relative Versus Absolute Scores   117
4.4 Results   119
    4.4.1 Media Effects Matter
        Relatively Little   123
    4.4.2 Use of Perspectives and Evidence 124
    4.4.3 Time on Task   125
    4.4.4 Complicating Factors   130
4.5 Summary   131

Chapter 5: Designing Better Online Learning
**   Environments**   **133**
5.1 The Challenge of Online Learning   133
5.2 Key Findings of this Research   134
    5.2.1 Conversational Dominance   136
    5.2.2 Quality of Discussion Content   139
    5.2.3 Efficiency of Conversational
        Medium   141
5.3 On Synchronicity   142
5.4 Implications for Designers   143
5.5 Future Directions   145

Appendix A: Discussion Topics and
**   Aggregated Answers**   **149**
A.1 Privacy and Blogs (Day 1)   149
A.2 Employees Accessing Private
    Information (Day 2)   161
    A.2.1 Scenario 1   161
    A.2.2 Scenario 2   168
A.3 Employee Monitoring (Day 3)   173

A.4 New Technologies for Law
    Enforcement (Day 4) 188
    A.4.1 Scenario 1 189
    A.4.2 Scenario 2 193

Appendix B: Discussion Transcripts **200**
    B.1 A "Good" Discussion 200
    B.2 A "Poor" Discussion 213

Notes **245**

References **249**

Index **269**

LIST OF FIGURES

Figure 1: Classroom Discussions with Profs.
Poulain and Sagnier   42

Figure 2: Online Discussions with Profs. Poulain
and Sagnier   42

Figure 3: Online and Classroom Interaction
Patterns   44

Figure 4: Comparing the Quality of
Discussion Content   120

LIST OF TABLES

Table 1: The Interaction Between Confidence
and Self-Awareness   74

Table 2: Medium Used in Each Class Session   106

Table 3: Details for Each Discussion   121

Table 4: Length of Conversations   125

FOREWORD

Some things are so familiar that they become invisible.
Consider this scenario: A teacher stands in front of a class
and lectures, stopping to ask questions now and then. Next,
he splits the class into small groups, and they discuss today's
topic. There is nothing unusual about this situation, except
that despite its familiarity, we still don't fully understand
it. It opens up a myriad of unanswered questions: Who is
speaking? The teacher? The students? How much for each?
Which students are speaking? The confident ones? The
shy ones? The ones who already knew the topic better?
The ones who hold mainstream opinions or more unusual
ones? If there are patterns here, why? And how does all
this affect what students are learning?

Technology enters the picture, and we have more questions
to ask. If students are talking online instead of face to face, how

is the situation different? Are the same people "speaking?" Are power relationships any different online, compared to face to face? Does participation in an online chat lead to learning in the same way as face to face? If the students are connecting from their dorm rooms or homes, are we even sure the quiet ones are really there?

These are not questions about technology—they are questions about learning in the presence of technology. As soon as we begin to try to answer these questions, we are just drawn back to our more basic questions: How do educational conversations work anyway? Studying learning in the presence of technology can be a catalyst for asking more fundamental questions about learning in general.

It takes a special skill set to study these kinds of issues—someone equally comfortable with technology and with learning, with qualitative methods and quantitative. And few people have mastered that range of skills as well as Jim Hudson. In this book, Jim applies those interdisciplinary talents to ask some important and fundamental questions. To shed light on things we rarely see because they are so familiar. Teachers, educational researchers, and educational technologists will all find this account interesting and useful, especially for the questions it asks.

Dr. Amy Bruckman
Associate Professor
College of Computing
Georgia Institute of Technology

PREFACE

Flame wars in newsgroups. Emotionally laden work emails. Employees fired over the contents of a personal blog. Every day, a lot of smart people say things online that they would never say face-to-face. From time to time, we all say things we regret, but if media reports are to be believed, this happens with alarming frequency online. The question is, why? Does it just take us a while to adjust to any new medium, or is there a deeper underlying cause? Can it be that the Internet changes the pscyhology of how we interact with one another?

As I have studied computer-mediated communication (CMC) over much of the last decade, I have come to believe that the design of new technology can profoundly alter the psychological state of the users of that technology. In other words, online behavior is fundamentally different from face-to-face behavior, and the design of Internet technologies is one of the leading factors underlying these differences. I have taken to calling this notion *technological pressure* because of its similarity to peer pressure. Like peer pressure, technological pressure pushes us to conform to a certain type of behavior, whether or not we are consciously aware of it. However, just like peer pressure, technological pressure is not the *cause* of behavior. We each ultimately bear individual responsibility for our actions, even in the face of external pressures. Technological pressure suggests that these forces act on us in powerful—and perhaps subsconscious—ways, but we still have the ability to freely choose our own behaviors.

Understanding how technological pressure works, however, is only the first step. By understanding how these psychological mechanisms operate in online environments, we can begin to develop new online environments that promote the types of behavior that we want. For example, if we are interested in uninhibited brainstorming, we might want to develop an environment that reduces the salience of power relationships (i.e., the boss vs. the employees). If we are looking to create a decision-making environment, however, we might want an environment that explicitly gives greater importance to the boss's comments. In order to consciously develop these types of environments, however, we need to know how the medium influences the behaviors that we care about.

In this book, I explore this theme by looking at how one particular type of technology—namely, text-based chat—influences educational discussions. I will show how features of the technology reduce inhibition, and encourage more equitable power distributions in educational discussions. Then, I will show how these changes have a relatively minor impact on the content of these discussions. Finally, I will conclude by using these findings to develop some specific design suggestions about how certain elements of online environments can be manipulated to encourage the types of behavior that we want to see.

ACKNOWLEDGMENTS

In looking back over the years of research that went into this book, it is difficult to find a way to thank all of those people who have played an important role in getting me to this point. With that in mind, I want to thank all of those who have contributed to my research over the years, especially those that I cannot name here. In particular, I want to thank the many teachers and students that have taken part in this research. Obviously, I could not have completed this book without you.

I must make mention of the student assistants that have helped with various stages of this research: Steve Jordan, Sharvari Nerukar, Dan Osiecki, PJ Packman, Craig Wampler, and James Yang. You have all been wonderful to work with, and I wish you the best as you pursue your own careers.

I also want to thank the graduate student colleagues with whom I discussed this research many, many times over the years. I could not have done this without Jason Elliott, Jochen "Je77" Rick, and the students in the Electronic Learning Communities (ELC) and Learning Sciences and Technologies (LST) research groups. Thank you for always being there for me—whether to challenge my research ideas or simply to let me vent. You have all been wonderful to work with.

My dissertation committee was also indispensable: Mark Guzdial, Janet Kolodner, Judy Olson, and Colin Potts. Mark, thanks for helping me translate my ideas into words that make sense. Janet, thank you for pushing me to achieve more, even when I didn't want to hear the feedback. Judy, thanks for pushing me toward a deeper methodological understanding. Colin, thank you for all of your help as I conducted the CS 4001 study.

I want to acknowledge the staff of the GVU Center for their support through the years. Your unceasing hard work behind the scenes has enabled everything that I have done. Without your help, this book would not be possible.

Without the individuals and companies that have provided me with financial support, it would have been much harder to get to this point. Study 1 was funded by an IBM Fellowship. Special thanks to Wendy Kellogg and Tom Erickson from IBM for their support. Study 2 was funded by a donation from Pitney Bowes. Special thanks to Austin Henderson and Jim Euchner from Pitney Bowes for this support.

Of course, there are also many who provided me with the emotional support needed. Gabriela Lopez, Ronda and Manuel Patino, and all of the students of Tango Rio have given me the right outlet through dance. Vi Nguyen-Tuong, Maitai, and Luna have provided unconditional love, even on the worst days. My parents—Mike and Janice Hudson—have always been there for me, telling me that I could become anything that I wanted.

Finally, I want to thank my advisor: Amy Bruckman. Without Amy's tireless support, I could not have gotten here today. Thank you for reading countless drafts of various documents, for pushing me to work harder, and for letting me follow different wild ideas.

Once again, I am grateful to all of you for all of your support through this process. Thank you.

ABBREVIATIONS

CMC   Computer-Mediated Communication
IRC   Internet Relay Chat
IRE   Initiate Respond Evaluate

CHATTING TO LEARN

CHAPTER 1

CHATROOMS AND LEARNING BEHAVIORS

1.1 THE CHALLENGES OF ONLINE LEARNING

For a number of reasons, online education is booming. Primary and secondary school students (Setzer, Lewis, & Greene, 2005), college students (I. E. Allen & Seaman, 2003, 2004), and corporate employees (Galvin, 2002) are all engaging more and more in some form of online or blended online/face-to-face education. The majority of college and university administrators in nearly every demographic segment agree that "online learning is critical to the long-term strategy" of their schools (I. E. Allen & Seaman, 2004, p. 2). Distance education universities, with enrollments in the hundreds of thousands, are beginning to venture into using online technologies to support learning (Daniel, 1996).

In the rush to move online, however, it is easy to forget that online education requires more than simply taking existing course materials and using them in this online medium. Even though online learning may superficially resemble a traditional face-to-face classroom, computer-mediated communication (CMC) technologies have different affordances than face-to-face communication, and these must be considered when designing online learning environments (Bruckman, 1999). A number of variables influence, in complex ways, educational success in the face-to-face classroom (Brown, 1992); online educational environments face the same challenges, but with a different set of variables.

The interaction of new and altered pedagogical variables makes the design of online learning environments complicated. For example, how does the choice of media influence educational discussions? What is the role/impact of discussion moderators? What is the influence of previous face-to-face interaction on the development of relationships and trust among the students? Do avatars convey necessary social cues, or do they get in the way of the ideas? Can photographs help promote team-oriented relationships or do they promote (perhaps subconscious) bias? As if these design choices were not challenging enough on their own, these choices interact in complicated ways with one another and with more traditional pedagogical choices (e.g., the design of educational activities).

Before rushing into online education, we need to better understand how to design appropriate online learning environments. Because of the complex interaction between design and pedagogical choices in online learning, research findings about the success of these environments have been, at best, mixed (Lou, Abrami, & d'Apollonia, 2001; M. Allen et al., 2004; Bernard et al., 2004). As a result of this "methodological morass," researchers have begun to call for a more systematic analysis of these variables and their interactions with one another (Bernard, Abrami, Lou, & Borokhovski, 2004). Just as the inappropriate use of educational technology in the classroom led some to call for a moratorium on spending until these types of issues are better understood (e.g., Cuban, 2001), we need to cautiously approach the use of online learning environments while we sort out the influence of these many new variables.

My research is an attempt to examine a small subset of these variables. Specifically, I explore how the choice of synchronous, text-based chat versus face-to-face interaction influences certain learning behaviors of college students in educational discussions. Through examining two learning domains, I show how changing conversational media influences—or does not influence—the resulting discussion among students who already knew one another from face-to-face interaction.

1.2 RESEARCH QUESTIONS

In this research, I explore one small aspect of the large constellation of variables affecting educational discussions. In particular, I focus on one particularly interesting

technology—text-based synchronous chat—and attempt
to understand how the choice of this medium influences
certain learning behaviors in small group discussions
among college students. Although there are many CMC
technologies that need to be explored, chat environments
are particularly interesting because the synchronicity of
this type of interaction resembles face-to-face classroom
discussions more closely than many other CMC technologies. One noteworthy feature of chat is that research has
shown that educational discussions in chatrooms tend to
be much more egalitarian than similar conversations in
face-to-face classrooms (Beauvois, 1992b; Kern, 1995;
Warschauer, 1997; Hudson & Bruckman, 2002). Specifically, this research has found that classroom conversations
are marked by instructor dominance, while online discussions have more student contributions compared with the
instructor. If we are going to use this knowledge to design
new online learning environments, though, we need to ask
why. What are the socio-technical features of chat discussions that encourage greater equity of participation? In
designing for *educational* discussions, we must further
ask about the efficacy of these environments. How do the
behavioral changes that occur in this online environment
affect the quality of the conversation?

To answer these research questions, I conducted two
studies. The first, in foreign language learning, looks at
a case study of two students interacting in a face-to-face
classroom and in an online chatroom. This study explores
some of the mechanisms that seem to lead to observed
behavioral changes when conversations move from one

medium to the other. The second study, in professional ethics education, uses a quasi-experimental design to determine how these behavioral changes influenced the content of small group discussions. Below, I describe each of these studies in more detail.

1.2.1 Conversational Equity: A Case Study

In the first study, I use a case study method (e.g., Yin, 2003) to examine some of the underlying mechanisms that lead students in foreign language learning situations to participate more in the online environment than they do in the face-to-face classroom. In this case study, I focus on two students—Christian and Sara—in a second-year college French class aimed at helping students integrate grammatical structures from previous classes into more fluent interaction. Christian was a confident senior who was raised in a country with a large French-speaking population. Although there was still room for improvement regarding his language abilities, he clearly was more fluent in French than the rest of the class. Not surprisingly, he talked relatively frequently in the face-to-face classroom. Sara, however, was a shy freshman who felt disadvantaged by having never visited a French-speaking country. She wanted to learn to speak the language, but was terrified of talking in front of the class. As such, she said nothing unless the instructor explicitly called on her to contribute.

When these two students began interacting online, however, things changed. Christian still talked a lot, but so did Sara! In fact, Sara was so comfortable that she actively, though politely, challenged the instructor's assumptions about important social issues. In this case study, I use the bystander effect—a social psychological theory of inhibition in emergency settings—as a lens for examining inhibition in the classroom and in the chatroom. Briefly, this approach suggests that there are some mechanisms that reduce inhibition in the online setting, and some that prohibit individuals from controlling the conversational floor. I describe this study in detail in Chapter 3.

1.2.2 Discussion Quality: A Quasi-Experimental Study

In the second study, I focus on understanding how these behavioral changes influence the content of group discussions. On one hand, we might hypothesize that reduced inhibition in chatrooms would encourage students to express and explore a greater variety of perspectives when engaging in debates surrounding social issues. On the other hand, there is also reason to believe that reduced inhibition might lead to anti-social behavior, which would effectively shut down rational discussion of issues. To explore this question, I conducted a quasi-experimental study in a professional ethics education environment.

For this study, I focused on two sections of a senior-level undergraduate course in professional ethics for computer scientists, which were taught by the same instructor. Over the course of four class periods, small groups of students met twice in the face-to-face classroom and twice in an online chatroom, which they could access from anywhere. I used a counter-balanced study design; on any given day, one class met online and the other met in the classroom. In this way, I obtained transcripts of discussion in both media on each discussion topic.

To analyze these data, I developed a coding scheme that examined how many perspectives each group used and how much evidence supported these perspectives. Using a procedure described in Chapter 4, I converted these codes into "grades" for each discussion, which could be compared with one another. Results indicate that discussions in the classroom and online both achieved similar quality scores. From group to group and day to day, however, there was a significant amount of variation. Results also indicate that efficiency was significantly reduced online; it took nearly twice as long for online students to achieve the same discussion quality as face-to-face students. This is described in more detail in Chapter 4.

1.3 LOOKING FORWARD

In Chapter 2, I present an overview of the relevant literature, divided into two parts. First, I describe research that has examined chat as a medium. Linguistic analysis, for example, shows that chat-based conversations contain some aspects of written language and some aspects of spoken language; they exist somewhere in between, as a separate and unique medium. Psychological research shows that these factors—which make chat environments unique—also lead to unexpected social behaviors, such as more equitable participation patterns.

Having looked at what makes chat a unique technology, Chapter 2 shifts focus to discuss educational research on those behaviors that I will explore in more detail in this book: equitable participation patterns and interaction quality. Research shows that equitable participation patterns are an important component of learning, but that various factors inhibit participation. Educational research also shows, however, that equitable participation patterns are necessary, but not sufficient, for learning. In order for discussions to be pedagogically useful, students must explore a variety of perspectives on a given issue and must learn to use evidence to support these perspectives.

Chapter 3 looks at understanding why chat environments seem to lead to greater equity of participation than face-to-face classrooms. Through looking at foreign language learning, I show that the initiate-respond-evaluate (IRE) cycle, which develops naturally in the classroom, does not seem to develop in the online environment. As a result, the instructor dominates classroom conversations, but online discussions have more equitable participation. I use an aspect of the social psychology literature—the bystander effect—as a lens to highlight some of the social and environmental cues that seem to influence this behavior. This chapter presents a case study of two students, and suggests some explanations for the patterns observed. In doing so, I provide evidence that properties of chat media influence power and dominance relationships through (a) changing the mechanisms normally used to control the conversational floor and (b) reducing inhibition levels in (normally) shy students.

Chapter 4 explores how these behavioral changes influence the quality of educational discussions. As one relevant measure of "quality," I focus on the content of group discussions in a professional ethics class. I present a quasi-experimental study that compares group discussions in the face-to-face classroom with similar discussions in an online chat environment. Although this study occurred in a naturalistic classroom setting, I was able to control many of the important variables. For example, this study involved two sections of the same class taught by one professor in the same semester. Students in these classes interacted in randomly assigned groups for four discussions. In each discussion, one section of the class met online while the other interacted in the classroom. Results from this study indicate that the medium has little impact on the quality of these educational discussions when compared with other factors, but that, in order to reach the same quality level, online conversations require twice the amount of time as face-to-face discussions.

The results of this research suggest that, when comparing chatrooms and face-to-face settings, group dynamics have a greater impact on the quality of educational discussions than has conversational medium. However, in some situations, chatrooms introduce some interesting new social dynamics through reducing certain inhibitions. For a number of reasons, it also seems that conversations in chatrooms require significantly more time than do face-to-face discussions. Chapter 5 takes these findings about chat and asks what they mean for designers of online environments, whether for education or for business. From a theoretical perspective, these findings emphasize that "synchronous" chat is not truly synchronous; there is some lag in the system that seems to have important pedagogical benefits. Based on these results, I suggest a number of design considerations.

CHAPTER 2

CHATROOMS AND SMALL GROUP LEARNING

2.1 CHATROOMS AND SMALL GROUP LEARNING

Before exploring how chatrooms influence behavior in educational discussions, it is useful to briefly examine the previous literature on each of these topics—that is, chatrooms and behavior in educational discussions—separately. First, I describe the literature on chatrooms and why they are an interesting medium for study. Although there is no theoretical reason for choosing chat over any other conversational medium, this technology is unique and interesting in a number of ways. After reviewing these features of the medium, I switch gears and focus on learning behaviors. As with any conversational media, there are a number of learning behaviors that text-based chat environments influence. Here, I show why two specific learning behaviors—conversational equity and the use of multiple perspectives with supporting evidence—are particularly interesting to study. After considering chat systems and learning behaviors relatively separately, I return to a discussion of what the literature says about using chatrooms to support educational discussions.

2.2 THE UNIQUENESS OF TEXT-BASED CHAT

From the earliest days of Internet-based communication, Unix systems have included a variant of the *talk* program. This program simply divides two users' computer terminals in half. Each user types in one half of the screen, and immediately sees the other user's keystrokes. Over time, the talk program evolved into *ytalk*, which allowed more than two users to communicate at one time. In 1988, Jarkko Oikarinen (n.d.) built on this idea to create Internet Relay Chat (IRC). Although Oikarinen points out that earlier chat programs existed, this is largely recognized as the beginning of Internet chat. Since Oikarinen developed this first IRC program, chat has evolved in a number of ways (e.g., Churchill, Trevor, Bly, & Nelson, 2000; Farnham, Chesley, McGhee, Kawal, & Landau, 2000; Erickson, Halverson, Kellogg, Laff, & Wolf, 2002; M. Smith, Cadiz, & Burkhalter, 2002), but the fundamental features have not significantly changed.

In text-based chat programs like IRC, a number of users can connect into the same virtual space and communicate with one another in near real time using text. Unlike *talk* and *ytalk*, IRC sends completed messages over the network, rather than individual keystrokes. In other words, most chat programs allow interlocutors to compose comments in private,[1] which are not revealed to others until the user presses the *Enter* key. In the conversation window, new comments are typically placed on the bottom of the screen when they arrive, causing older messages to be pushed up and eventually scrolled off the top of the screen.

Although there are some resemblances to other communication media, text-based chat technologies represent a new form of interaction. In the next sections, I describe two lines of research that have attempted to understand how this new medium changes interaction. First, I present results from linguistic analyses that have illustrated ways that this type of interaction relates to interaction in other media. Then, I focus on literature exploring new behavioral patterns that arise in online chat.

2.2.1 Linguistic Features of Chat Conversations

Due to the fact that chat messages are composed before being displayed, the usual turn-taking mechanisms that provide for an orderly conversation (Grice, 1975) break down. Chat messages appear in the temporal order that the chat server receives them; several conversational turns may occur between a comment and its response. Because there are no mechanisms for the orderly exchange of the conversational floor, threads of discussion tend to interleave in chat environments (Werry, 1996). Although this has led many to speculate about the difficulties that can arise from these new threading structures (e.g., Farnham, Chesley, McGhee, Kawal, & Landau, 2000; M. Smith, Cadiz, & Burkhalter, 2002), reports of smaller group discussions (i.e., composed of less than about 15 people) rarely identify this as a problem (e.g., McDaniel, Olson, & Magee, 1996). For example, in conducting my research with a number of college students in multiple learning domains, no one reported problems with conversational threading. Herring (1999), having analyzed this lack of interactional coherence related to threading structures, suggests that the popularity of chat in spite of this limitation may have to do with the new types of linguistic play enabled, such as the ability to participate in multiple "conversations" at once.

The linguistic structure of chat interaction tends to look somewhat like that of face-to-face interaction (Condon & Cech, 1996), but with some notable exceptions. Because of the reduced efficiency involved in typing, chat conversations typically omit unnecessary linguistic information, such as some grammatical structures and elaborations/ repeats of ideas (Condon & Cech, 1996). Similarly interlocutors in a chatroom rely heavily on abbreviations (Werry, 1996), which often serve as linguistic markers to identify membership in the in-group (Wenger, 1998; Cherny, 1999; Sassenberg, 2002). Although there is some evidence to suggest that this type of linguistic play may be an important component of identity development more generally (Bruce, Peyton, & Batson, 1993; Turkle, 1995; Merchant, 2001), this is beyond the scope of this book.

2.2.2 Behavioral Features of Chat Conversations

Of the many changes that occur when conversations take place in text-based chatrooms, *disinhibition* holds some of the most interesting implications for the design of new learning environments for education. Briefly, there is considerable evidence to suggest that behaviors in chatrooms and other online environments tend to be less constrained by social inhibitions when compared with interaction in other media (Kiesler, Siegel, & McGuire, 1984; Lea & Spears, 1991; Joinson, 1998; Postmes & Spears, 1998; Spears, Lea, & Postmes, 2001; Joinson, 2003). Online, interlocutors tend to be less aware of power hierarchies (Dubrovsky, Kiesler, & Sethna, 1991; Sproull & Kiesler, 1991). They tend to reveal much more personal information than in other media (Weisband & Kiesler, 1996; Joinson, 2001a, 2001b; Tidwell & Walther, 2002). They provide help in more altruistic ways (Kollock & Smith, 1996; Kollock, 1999; Markey, 2000).

Throughout this book, I look at the implications of disinhibition for educational discussions. On the one hand, disinhibition in educational chat environments seems to lead to greater equity (Sproull & Kiesler, 1991; Beauvois, 1997; Warschauer, 1997) and increased intellectual risk-taking (Kern, 1995; Pellettieri, 2000). On the other hand, there is evidence that disinhibition easily leads to negative forms of interaction, such as flaming (Dery, 1993; Joinson, 2003). Before dealing with the implications of disinhibition, however, it is useful to review one of the current theories of why these behavioral changes occur. In Chapter 3, I will build on this theory and show how a new approach to explaining these behaviors can provide useful design suggestions in the development of new online environments.

2.2.2.1 Self-Awareness

Much of the research on inhibition in small group environments has focused on self-awareness. In the original formulation, Duval and Wicklund (1972) posited that there are two dimensions to self-awareness. The awareness of how others perceive and judge an individual is called *public self-awareness,* while the awareness of one's own goals and motivations is termed *private self-awareness.*[2] This concept has been especially important in describing changes in inhibition that appear to be caused by the conversational medium itself (e.g., Kiesler, Siegel, & McGuire, 1984; Matheson & Zanna, 1988; Hudson & Bruckman, 2004).

Because they are orthogonal concepts, private and public self-awareness can impact inhibition independently. According to the theory (Duval & Wicklund, 1972), when public self-awareness decreases, individuals become less concerned about the judgments of others, and will behave in less inhibited ways. Private self-awareness, however, works in the opposite way. When private self-awareness increases, individuals become focused more exclusively on their own goals and motivations. Therefore, *decreased* public self-awareness and *increased* private self-awareness both lead to greater disinhibition.

Based on this theory, Kiesler, Siegel, and McGuire (1984) suggested that changes in self-awareness might explain the propensity toward more equitable interaction in online environments. To test this theory, Matheson and Zanna (1988) had groups of students perform a conjunctive experimental task, and then fill out a survey measuring public and private self-awareness. The survey metric [(Prentice-Dunn & Rogers, 1982 based on Fenigstein, Scheier & Buss, 1975)] aimed to separate individually varying, situation-independent self-awareness (i.e., chronic self-awareness) from more global, situation-dependent self-awareness (i.e., acute self-awareness). Results from this study indicate that small group interaction in online environments induces higher levels of acute private self-awareness, while marginally lowering public self-awareness (Matheson & Zanna, 1988). In other words, individuals in online environments seem to be much more aware of their own motivations, and a little less concerned about what others think. There is suggestive evidence from other studies, however, that public self-awareness is lowered in online environments when power hierarchies, such as teacher-student relationships, are present (e.g., Kern, 1995; Hudson & Bruckman, 2004), perhaps because of increased public self-awareness in these face-to-face environments.

There is also evidence that confidence levels mediate the relationship between public self-awareness and inhibition. Public self-awareness seems to interact with confidence through a process termed *social facilitation* (Zajonc, 1965; Bond & Titus, 1983). Specifically, highly confident students tend to perform better when they have high public self-awareness (i.e., when they are observed by others). Low confidence students, however, do better when public self-awareness is low (i.e., when they are not observed by others). I will return to this theme in Chapter 3 where I suggest that the interaction between these variables—self-confidence and public self-awareness—can lead low confidence students to speak significantly more in an online environment than in a classroom environment.

2.3 IMPORTANT LEARNING BEHAVIORS

Having looked at the unique features of chat environments, I now shift my focus to the learning behaviors that seem particularly relevant for the study of these environments. As I described in Chapter 1, there are a number of pedagogical decisions and design variables that influence learning. By studying the interaction of a small set of these variables, we can improve our understanding of the design of new educational technologies. In this section, I describe two learning behaviors that seem to be especially salient in chat conversations: conversational equity and the reasoned exploration of multiple perspectives.

2.3.1 The Importance of Conversational Equity

By now, it is generally accepted that small group learning can have pedagogical benefits that surpass those achieved through individual learning (Lou, Abrami, & d'Apollonia, 2001), but there is still debate about the appropriate conditions for ideal small group learning. In reviewing the literature on small group discussions in the classroom, Cohen (1994) highlights a potential contradiction in identifying factors that promote learning. In her own research on Complex Instruction (e.g., E. G. Cohen, 1984; E. G. Cohen & Lotan, 1995), Cohen has demonstrated that simple measures of on-topic interaction usually correlate with learning gains. In a series of studies on mathematics learning, however, Webb (1991) has shown that on-topic interaction plays only a minor role when compared with the importance of giving and receiving detailed explanations.

To resolve this conflict, Cohen (1994) hypothesizes that the task structure seems to play an important role in determining the relative importance of different behaviors in group learning. In his work on group processes, Steiner (1972) described three types of group tasks: additive, conjunctive, and disjunctive. In additive tasks, all group members perform the same task, and then pool their results. In conjunctive tasks, each group member must uniquely contribute to achieving the group goal. In other words, performance of the group often depends largely on the performance of the weakest member of the group. Disjunctive tasks, however, depend on the strongest member of the group, because they are tasks that require only one individual to identify the best answer (although the other group members must still accept this answer).

Cohen used conjunctive tasks in her studies while Webb focused more on disjunctive tasks. She argues that the outcome of conjunctive tasks depends primarily on interaction, and that the outcome of disjunctive tasks depends on explanation (E. G. Cohen, 1994). Chizhik's (2001) research on the relationship between social status and task type offers supporting evidence for Cohen's hypothesis. Specifically, he examined small groups of students—containing one Caucasian male, one Caucasian female, one African-American male, and one African-American female—performing either a conjunctive or a disjunctive task. Although he found evidence confirming Cohen's hypothesis about the importance of on-topic interaction, Chizhik also suggests that social status differentials can inhibit interaction. In other words, he found that group members with higher social status tend to dominate the discussion. Since the research described above on chatrooms suggests that this medium seems to have a direct impact on levels of inhibition and social status, it makes sense to examine, in a more detailed way, how social status affects classroom interaction.

2.3.1.1 Social Status and Inhibition

Whether based on race (e.g., Chizhik, 1999, 2001; Nye, Hedges, & Konstantopoulos, 2004), gender (e.g., Hsi & Hoadley, 1997; Mistler-Jackson & Songer, 2000; Sussman & Tyson, 2000), physical attractiveness (e.g., Webster & Driskell, 1983; Anderson, John, Keltner, & Kring, 2001; Kanazawa & Kovar, 2004), popularity (e.g., Wright, Giammarino, & Parad, 1986; E. G. Cohen, Lotan, Scarloss, & Arellano, 1999; Lease, Musgrove, & Axelrod, 2002), explicit power relationships (e.g., Dubrovsky, Kiesler, & Sethna, 1991; France, Anderson, & Gardner, 2001), or academic ability (e.g., Dembo & McAuliffe, 1987; Lloyd & Cohen, 1999), differences in social status within small groups can often affect the equity of interaction[3] (Levine & Moreland, 1998). Group members with higher social status tend to talk more than those with lower social status. Moreover, group members generally accept this as the way that things should be.

In a classic study of this affect, Dembo and McAuliffe (1987) gave a group of students a fictional test called the "California Test of Problem-Solving Ability," and told the students that it predicted how well they would do on a subsequent conjunctive task. Then, students were randomly divided into groups. Ten of the groups (with four students each) were told that, according to the test, they all had average aptitude for the type of problem they were about to solve. The other ten groups were told that two particular students had high ability while the other two only possessed average ability. In those groups with mixed "ability" levels, the higher status students spoke more, took more initiative in offering advice and feedback to low-status students, and had more influence on group decisions. Randomly assigned status hierarchies significantly impacted on group processes.

As the Dembo and McAuliffe study illustrates, social status is complex, and status hierarchies form quickly—typically within minutes (Levine & Moreland, 1998). Often, these status hierarchies are based on proximal characteristics[4] of social status such as academic ability and institutional power hierarchies, which can outweigh the influence of more distal characteristics such as race and gender (E. G. Cohen, Lotan, Scarloss, & Arellano, 1999). When multiple measures of social status conflict, evidence suggests that more equitable patterns of participation can emerge (Lloyd & Cohen, 1999). For example, a student who is not academically gifted, but who is quite popular is just as likely to talk in a small group as the student who academically excels, but remains relatively unpopular.

Lloyd and Cohen (1999) note that significant problems arise for those students who are low in both peer and academic status, and for those students placed in groups with too wide status differentials.

Research on new technologies for collaboration has shown that media choice can also play an important role in leveling social hierarchies. In the late 1970s, Hiltz and Turoff (1978) hypothesized that computer technology might alleviate many of the social status effects because of reduced social cues online. During the 1980s and early 1990s, a flurry of research activity confirmed this hypothesis (e.g., Kiesler, Siegel, & McGuire, 1984; Dubrovsky, Kiesler, & Sethna, 1991; Sproull & Kiesler, 1991). In the past decade, research has focused on developing a more nuanced picture of when and why social hierarchies change online (e.g., Joinson, 1998; Wallace, 1999; Bargh, McKenna, & Fitzsimons, 2002; Joinson, 2003; Hudson & Bruckman, 2004). This research has found that social status effects largely disappear in text-based environments, unlike audio- and video-based environments (France, Anderson, & Gardner, 2001; Huang, Olson, & Olson, 2002).

In Chapter 3, I offer a new way of looking at these behavioral changes. This approach—the bystander effect—draws on my experiences in using chat to support foreign language learning (Hudson & Bruckman, 2001, 2002). In the next section, I describe some of the features of foreign language learning that made it an interesting domain in which to explore the causes and design implications of these behavioral changes.

2.3.1.2 An Interesting Domain:
Foreign Language Learning
Social status differentials tend to inhibit lower-status individuals from participating equally in educational discussions, which can have detrimental effects on learning. However, chat environments seem to correct much of this imbalance. The question is: why? Which social psychological mechanisms contribute? In Chapter 3, I describe a case study of two students interacting in a French classroom. In this section, I describe some of the features of foreign language learning that makes this an interesting domain for studying the problems of participation.

Most researchers and educators can agree that learning a foreign language as an adult is difficult, particularly when compared with child language learning. Fewer, however, agree on the reasons, although the critical period hypothesis has received notable attention. In its simplest form, this hypothesis argues that something changes in the brain in late childhood or around puberty that causes adults to approach foreign languages differently from native language(s) (Scovel, 2000). In other words, a child learns all languages in the same manner, but an adult—having already learned his or her native language—learns through different processes. Although the exact age and nature of this change are still debated, the core of the argument rests on the belief that there is something fundamentally different between the ways adults and young (enough) children approach language learning.

The language ego permeability hypothesis, however, presents a different—though compatible—picture of this learning difficulty. Unlike the critical period hypothesis, the language ego permeability theory argues that changes largely result from socialization rather than maturation. This hypothesis starts from the understanding that an individual will present different aspects of his or her self, depending on how he or she wishes others to perceive the interaction (Goffman, 1963, 1967; Ornstein & Ehrlich, 1989). By adulthood, many individuals are quite adept at presenting the "appropriate" image of themselves in any situation. Whether this is consciously or unconsciously done, all people engage in this type of behavior in nearly every interaction.

Learning a foreign language as an adult requires that the individual give up the control over the self-presentation that language use can provide. Since individuals do not have the same control over a foreign language as over their native languages, they become inhibited about using the new language (Guiora, 1972). They fear making mistakes, even though they are an important part of the learning process (Kolodner, 1997). Therefore, adults do not receive the practice necessary to reach linguistic fluency. Unlike the critical period hypothesis, this view allows for the variation that is seen in ultimate levels of adult achievement. If it were true that foreign language fluency is impossible for adults to obtain, we would not have the masterful works of English literature written by Joseph Conrad or Vladimir Nabokov.

Although the critical period hypothesis is likely to have some considerable degree of validity, the language ego permeability theory explains the same phenomena and also contains a number of implications for improving the foreign language education experience. Most importantly, it suggests that inhibition plays a powerful role in constraining achievement. To study the role of inhibition in the foreign language learning process, Guiora and his colleagues developed the Standard Thai Procedure,[5] a method designed to elicit oral production measures from students learning to speak words in a distant foreign language in which they have had no previous exposure. Essentially, students listen to a tape that asks them to repeat words in Thai—a language with little similarity to English. Students are also screened to ensure no previous exposure to the Thai language. Finally, researchers code the samples for similarity to native speaker pronunciation.

Using this procedure, researchers have explored the role of inhibition in the learning process by comparing results from students acting normally and from students under the influence of inhibition-lowering drugs, namely alcohol and valium. In each of these studies, all students participated in the Standard Thai Procedure. Only the experimental group received the drug while the control group received a placebo. In the experiments using alcohol (Guiora, Beit-Hallahmi, Brannon, Dull, & Scovel, 1972), they found clear evidence that moderate amounts of alcohol insignificantly lowered mental reasoning, while significantly improving oral production skills. Studies with valium (Guiora, Acton, Erard, & Strickland, 1980) and hypnosis (Schumann, Holroyd, Campbell, & Ward, 1978) found similar, though not as strong, results. Although this is interesting evidence, it suffers from two weaknesses. First, oral production in an unfamiliar, distant language does not generalize well to other language learning skills. Second, these types of techniques for lowering inhibition offer little in terms of practical classroom teaching methods. A number of techniques for dealing with inhibition have arisen, but few have been adopted. Inhibition still offers a challenge to the language learning process.

In a separate body of literature, however, various CMC technologies have been credited with having the ability to lower inhibitions among those online (e.g., Joinson, 1998; Spears, Lea, & Postmes, 2001). If CMC lowers inhibitions, and if inhibition difficulties are particularly salient challenges in the domain of language learning, it makes sense that students in an online environment might overcome these difficulties. In fact, this has been demonstrated by a number of researchers examining chat environments for foreign language learning (Beauvois, 1992b; Kelm, 1992; Bruce, Peyton, & Batson, 1993; Kern, 1995; Beauvois, 1997).

In 1985, text-based chat environments first found their way into the classroom as a tool for foreign language education. This effort began as a way of helping deaf children learn English through the Electronic Networks for Interaction (ENFI) project (Batson, 1993). Since deaf children only experience English in its written form, they never have the opportunity to explore playful interaction through the language. To them, English is often a fixed, boring language. Motivation to learn the language is difficult to impart to these students. The ENFI project sought to provide playful, English-based interactions in a forum that could easily include the deaf students. Since ENFI conversations are both written and synchronous, deaf students were able to use the medium to actively play with the language. As a result, dramatic improvements in motivation to learn were observed (Bruce, Peyton, & Batson, 1993). The deaf children seemed to thrive in this type of foreign language learning environment.

With the success of chat for deaf language education, a number of other foreign language educators began to look at the use of synchronous, text-based interactions for other types of language students (e.g., Beauvois, 1992b; Kelm, 1992). Even though students of other languages must contend with speech in addition to writing, these researchers believed that text-based chat could still play a positive role. Much of this early research on chat for foreign language learning focused on explaining its role in language learning environments and pedagogies. The largest body of literature looks at shifting power and dominance relations between individuals. It is now widely accepted in the foreign language learning literature, that chat-based online discussions can have a much more democratic quality, with instructors speaking significantly less than they do in the classroom (e.g., Kern, 1995). Not only are teacher/ student interactions often more balanced, but there is also some evidence to suggest that gender equity increases in the online environment (Wang & Hurst, 1997).

A number of these studies have taken closer looks at the affective components of the online interactions. In these online environments, students exhibit higher levels of attention (Beauvois, 1992b). They are more honest and candid toward those in a position of authority (Kelm,

1992). They get to know one another much better online than in the classroom environment (Beauvois, 1997). Language use is more extensive and more advanced online than in the classroom (Kern, 1995). Students tend to speak in the foreign language; code switches into the native language—even among participants who share a common native language—are relatively rare (Beauvois, 1992a; Kelm, 1992; Kern, 1995). The student experience in the online environment is different from the experience in the classroom, particularly with regard to feelings of (less) dominance and inhibition.[6]

Further, language ego permeability theory implies that the greater linguistic output demonstrated by the students in the online environment has effects beyond those that could be attributed to greater time on task. The fact that the output exhibits greater disinhibition contributes to language learning. By partially overcoming this barrier to language learning, online environments likely provide not only increased, but also more effective language practice. Language production in an environment marked by lower inhibition likely contributes toward deeper learning rather than simply toward greater time on task. Although there is some evidence that oral language skills improve through this type of text-based activity (Payne & Whitney, 2002; Payne & Ross, 2005), further research into learning outcomes in online chat environments is needed (Ortega, 1997).

2.3.2 The Importance of Perspective Taking
In the last section, I discussed how Chizhik's (2001) work on social status in conjunctive versus disjunctive

conversations supports Cohen's (1994) claim that the amount of on-topic interaction is an important predictor of positive outcomes for conjunctive group tasks. His work, however, also suggests that the type of on-topic interaction matters. In particular, the literature on group interaction suggests that it is important for students to take on multiple perspectives and to use certain types of evidence and logic to support these perspectives.

Based on their research on intellectual conflict in educational settings, Johnson and Johnson (1988; 2000) developed a pedagogical approach to cooperative learning that they term *academic controversy*. In academic controversy, two pairs of students comprise a four-person group. Each pair is assigned either a pro or a con position on some issue, and the instructor provides the entire group with a resource packet containing balanced evidence for each perspective. After using these materials to prepare, the pairs of students enter into debate with each other by advocating their assigned position. After a specified period of time, the students switch perspectives and discuss the topic again. Once both sides have taken each perspective, the four-person group must agree on a single position and create a written artifact.

In over thirty years of research, Johnson and Johnson (2000; Johnson, Johnson, & Smith, 2000) have found consistent evidence that this pedagogical approach leads to significant gains over traditional methods of consensus-seeking, debate, or individual learning.[7] Specifically, this work has suggested that the process of taking multiple perspectives leads to improved elaboration of ideas (K. A. Smith,

Johnson, & Johnson, 1984), improved learning of academic material (Mitchell, Johnson, & Johnson, 2002), and more creative problem solutions (K. A. Smith, Petersen, Johnson, & Johnson, 1986). In fact, Johnson and Johnson have extended this work into conflict management education, where they have shown similar learning benefits associated with training students to see an issue from multiple points of view (Stevahn, Johnson, Johnson, & Schultz, 2002).

To achieve these learning outcomes, Johnson and Johnson (1988) emphasize several important conditions. At an environmental level, they stress that conflict must occur in a setting where students demonstrate that they value one another, even if they disagree intellectually. At the group level, they suggest that heterogeneous groups are more likely to engender intellectual disagreement. This is also in keeping with Cohen's (1994) findings. At the process level, Johnson and Johnson point out that groups should (a) be given access to information that provides balanced evidence for each perspective, and (b) engage in cycles of differentiation (i.e., elaborating and clarifying hypotheses and evidence) and integration (i.e., combining perspectives and generating creative solutions).

Academic controversy, however, is not without limitations. Although research on this pedagogical technique has provided ample evidence that focusing on multiple perspectives is an important component of learning (Johnson & Johnson, 2000; Johnson, Johnson, & Smith, 2000), this research does not compare academic controversy with less structured, but controversy-oriented group discussion techniques. Because of this and other[8] methodological limitations, it is impossible to draw specific conclusions about the effectiveness of this technique when compared with other pedagogical approaches that also focus on the role of perspective-taking and elaboration of ideas (e.g., Bell, Davis, & Linn, 1995).

Collaboration scripts, such as Johnson and Johnson's academic controversy or Palincsar and Brown's (1984) reciprocal teaching, are well learned interaction patterns that serve to scaffold group work (O'Donnell & Dansereau, 1992). Although there is sufficient evidence to suggest that collaboration scripts can encourage learning, Dillenbourg (2002) warns against too much reliance on scripts. He fears that the use of collaboration scripts—especially scripts reified in technology—might "drift away from the genuine notion of collaborative learning, ... [removing] the fun and richness of group interactions" (Dillenbourg, 2002, p. 61). Rituals in Kolodner's Learning By Design (Kolodner et al., 2003) also perform the same function as collaboration scripts, but with much more flexibility in the details of interaction. In these rituals, students routinely engage in ritualized forms of communication in which they reflect on their own ideas and prompt one another for greater elaboration (Kolodner & Gray, 2002).

2.3.2.1 An Interesting Domain:
Professional Ethics Education
How do these forms of less structured argumentation play out in online chat environments? This remains an open research question. The disinhibition observed in these environments, might lead us to conclude that greater

equity in participation might lead students with minority viewpoints to feel more comfortable expressing these opinions. However, it is equally possible that disinhibition will lead to reduced elaboration, as students express their positions without seriously engaging one another in argumentation. In Chapter 4, I describe a quasi-experimental study of the impact of medium choice (i.e., chat versus face-to-face) on these behaviors, using discussions in a professional ethics class. Here, I describe the motivation for focusing on this learning domain.

In many ways, applied ethics courses have the goal of exploring multiple perspectives with well-reasoned supporting evidence. In his work on discourse ethics, Habermas (1993) suggested that social groups can arrive at certain universal principles of behavior through a process of argumentation that (1) respects each individual as having a valid perspective that is worthy of consideration and (2) grounds itself on validity claims that can be criticized and challenged. In his own words:

> Discourse ethics prefers to view shared understanding about the generalizability of interests as the *result* of an intersubjectively mounted *public discourse*. There are no shared structures preceding the individual except the universals of language use. (Habermas, 1990, p. 203, emphasis in original)

Since universal principles are built on public discourse, Habermas (1962) further suggested that these principles are open to reanalysis and reinterpretation. Social norms can and do change over time, requiring continual discussion and reevaluation.

College-level professional ethics courses are typically explicitly designed to help students recognize ethical situations, and to provide them with the argumentation skills that they need in order to participate in this type of discourse surrounding the social issues that affect their professions (Callahan, 1980; Callahan & Bok, 1980; M. Keefer & Ashley, 2001). Course goals focus both on helping students respect one another's opinions, and on giving them the argumentation skills to explore the validity of these perspectives in an open-minded way. In Chapter 4, I will look at the use of perspectives and evidence in classroom and online discussions in one particular professional ethics class at Georgia Tech.

2.4 LEARNING WITH TECHNOLOGY

As this review of the literature on small group interaction has demonstrated, the choice of medium can play an important role in determining the type of conversation that results. In particular, we know that online environments can level the social playing field (e.g., Dubrovsky, Kiesler, & Sethna, 1991; Sproull & Kiesler, 1991), reduce inhibition (e.g., Lea & Spears, 1991; Joinson, 1998; Freiermuth, 2001; Joinson, 2003), and increase motivation (e.g., Beauvois, 1994/1995; Songer, 1996; Mistler-Jackson & Songer, 2000). However, we know much less about how these medium-induced changes affect the quality of the interaction that results. In fact, a significant amount of literature, especially early studies of social interaction online, has illustrated a number of negative interaction cycles that can emerge (e.g., Walther, 1992; Dery, 1993; Walther & Anderson, 1994).

A recent review of the literature comparing online, distance education with more traditional classroom education points to a number of challenges in drawing conclusions about the quality of interaction online (Bernard et al., 2004). The review found wide variance in learning outcomes, which masked any real differences between classroom and online environments that may have been present. When the distance education environments were subdivided into studies using synchronous technologies, and those studies using asynchronous technologies, some differences emerged. In general, students learning through synchronous technologies performed more poorly than students in the classroom. Students in the classroom, in turn, performed worse than those using asynchronous technologies. Nevertheless, there was significant variance in all conditions, and the sizes of the effects were relatively small.

A separate meta-analysis, however, arrived at the opposite conclusion (M. Allen et al., 2004). Although this review found a slight edge for both synchronous and asynchronous systems over face-to-face education, a large amount of variance made interpretation difficult. Similarly, research on group support systems (GSS) in collaborative work has shown no significant difference between face-to-face and online systems, with high variance (Fjermestad & Hiltz, 1998–1999). A number of reviewers have noted that methodological limitations in many of these studies have hindered the conclusions that can be drawn (Fjermestad & Hiltz, 1998–1999; Bernard, Abrami, Lou, & Borokhovski, 2004).

In attempting to make sense of the heterogeneity of these findings, it is important to remember that technologies which are successful in one environment (e.g., Rick, Guzdial, Carroll, Holloway-Attaway, & Walker, 2002) are often unsuccessful in another (e.g., Guzdial et al., 2001); a number of social and environmental factors significantly influence the success of new technology (Guzdial & Carroll, 2002). In order to design more productive learning environments, we need to ask questions about how and why design decisions affect learning behaviors. Although we are making progress at understanding how to appropriately apply CMC technologies to educational settings, more is needed. In the next two chapters, I explore how the choice of text-based chat environments influences learning behaviors in open-ended (i.e., conjunctive) educational discussions.

CHAPTER 3

EXPLAINING EQUITY:
A CASE STUDY

3.1 QUESTIONING THE CAUSES OF BEHAVIORAL CHANGES

In the last chapter, I described research that shows how power and dominance relationships change when conversations move from face-to-face settings to online chatrooms. There is significant evidence that interlocutors of different social status tend to interact more equitably in chatrooms than they do in face-to-face environments (e.g., Sproull & Kiesler, 1991; Joinson, 1998; Wallace, 1999; Warschauer, 1999; Joinson, 2003). If we are going to use these findings to design better learning environments, however, we need to better understand the mechanisms that lead to these behavioral changes. Why do chat environments seem to encourage greater equity of participation, especially by those individuals of differing social status? In this chapter, I use a social psychological theory of inhibition in emergency settings—the bystander effect (Latané & Darley, 1970)—as a new lens for viewing inhibition in educational settings. Using a case study method (Yin, 2003), I show how this new lens helps highlight salient behaviors in each environment and leads to a number of specific design considerations.

First, however, it is useful to look in a little more detail at the participation patterns that arise in educational chatrooms. This effect has been particularly salient in foreign language learning settings, where participation in discussions is crucial. This research has shown that conversations in foreign language learning chatrooms tend to have much greater student interaction, and that teachers have reduced conversational dominance (Beauvois, 1992b; Kelm, 1992; Beauvois, 1997; Warschauer, 1997). This change is accompanied by a greater willingness by students to take linguistic risks in attempting to integrate new grammatical structures and vocabulary (Kern, 1995). Further, research has also shown that there is reason to believe that interaction in text-based chatrooms can help improve oral pronunciation and verbal fluency (Payne & Whitney, 2002; Payne & Ross, 2005). My own work with IRC Français—a chat program designed specifically to support foreign language learning outside of the computer lab (Hudson & Bruckman, 2002)—revealed similar changes in conversational dominance. In the next section, I describe my observations with IRC Français to better illustrate these changing participation patterns. Afterwards, I describe a case study of two students and show how using the bystander effect as a lens can lead to new design considerations.

3.2 PATTERNS OF PARTICIPATION IN FOREIGN LANGUAGE LEARNING

During spring semester of 2000, I involved four second-year college French classes from two different universities in a study that compared classroom participation patterns with those in IRC Français, a chat tool that I developed specifically to support the unique needs of foreign language students seeking to practice their language skills over the internet (Hudson & Bruckman, 2002). As part of the class, each student had to converse online for one hour each week in a scheduled chat session, which was hosted by an instructor. Although each teacher hosted one session each week, students were not required to attend their teacher's session. Instead, students were welcome to attend any of the scheduled chats with any host. At these scheduled sessions, hosts were given responsibility for determining how to control the flow of conversation. Just like a host at a party, the style of hosting a conversation should reflect the individual's personality (Rheingold, 1993). Therefore, I informed the hosts from the beginning that they should maintain the conversation in whatever manner seemed most appropriate. I encouraged the individuality of our hosts and supported them as the foundation of community building. As such, topics were sometimes drawn from classroom discussions, such as "recount a dream (*raconter un rêve*)." Other times, the topics are drawn from events in everyday life, such as "love: the good, the bad, and the ugly (*l'amour: le bon, le mauvais, et le laid*)" around Valentine's Day.

Over the course of the semester, I randomly videotaped the classroom conversations with two of the instructors— one at each university. Afterwards, I chose representative classroom sessions for transcription and further analysis; based on my experience with these classes and with these instructors in previous semesters, I chose to examine transcripts in which the classes carried out whole-group discussions on topic. At the end of the semester, I chose five students and three teachers for in-depth interviews. Below, I present data about interactions involving these two teachers as a way of comparing the online and offline discussions.

3.2.1 Conversational Dynamics
One student described her classroom interactions:

> [The teacher] talks most of the time, actually. Literally, I maybe get in two to three sentences in class of me actually speaking. [...] It's a bit awkward sometimes because she'll pose these questions. It's supposed to be a free forum for anyone to answer and try to get a discussion started. Maybe we're just not comfortable enough with each other yet to actually do that. So, everyone just kind of sits there and she'll go around the circle prompting you to respond to the question.

Everyone takes their seven seconds in the limelight and says something. And that's it.

The classroom—even with good teachers—often follows a pattern that plays out in many educational settings. The teacher enters the room with a question prepared. Hopefully, this question will generate discussion that the teacher can use to explore the learning goals of the day. When the teacher asks this question, however, all eye contact ceases. Students stare at the floor, at their books, at anything to keep from being called on. Faced with this wall of silence, the teacher must eventually pick a "victim" and call on him or her. That student, then, has a mini-conversation with the teacher. Satisfied with the answer, the teacher moves on to another student, as the first breathes a sigh of relief. This pattern has often been referred to as the Initiate-Respond-Evaluate (IRE) cycle (Newman, Griffin, & Cole, 1989). The teacher initiates the discussion. The student responds to the teacher. The teacher evaluates the response. Figure 1 shows the word count for the teachers and students in this type of participation pattern.

As Figure 2 and Figure 3 show, however, this cycle breaks down when conversations move online. The teacher still initiates the discussion, but multiple students respond. Rather than waiting for a teacher to evaluate them, students continue responding to one another. In the dialog that forms, the teacher becomes just another participant. The teacher still has an important voice in the conversation, but no longer mediates between the students. Students actively respond to one another and take the discussion in directions that they find interesting.

Figure 1. Classroom Discussions with Profs. Poulain and Sagnier

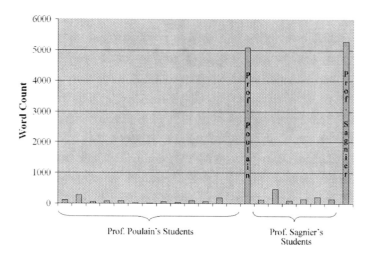

Figure 2. Online Discussions with Profs. Poulain and Sagnier

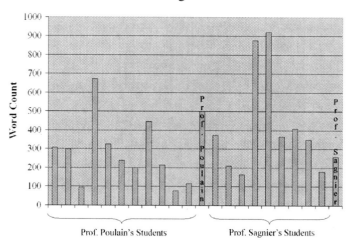

For example, student assumption of conversational control was particularly salient in one conversation during this study. In the interviews with students, many commented that the worst conversation they had online was one about Parisian architecture. However, when I went back and examined this conversation, nearly every student commented at the end that it was one of the best conversations they had ever had. Clearly, the same individuals describing the same event do not often use both "best" and "worst." Examining the conversation more closely revealed the source of the contradiction. At the beginning of the conversation, the teacher, Prof. Sagnier,[9] introduced the topic of Parisian architecture.[10] After some discussion, the students explicitly (though politely) told her that they were bored with the topic. It was too much like something in a textbook. Accepting this, Prof. Sagnier asked for suggestions of a different topic. One student from Haiti offered to share his knowledge and experiences with Haitian voodoo monuments. The students spent the rest of the conversation exploring this individual's culture. Because students felt comfortable telling the teacher that they did not find a topic engaging, what started as the worst conversation ended up becoming the best conversation that they remembered.

When conversations move online, participation patterns change significantly. In the following sections, I present details from the two teachers we observed. Because these two teachers at different institutions exhibit changes similar to those documented in other studies (e.g., Beauvois, 1994/1995; Kern, 1995), I believe that these changes are

Figure 3. Online and Classroom Interaction Patterns

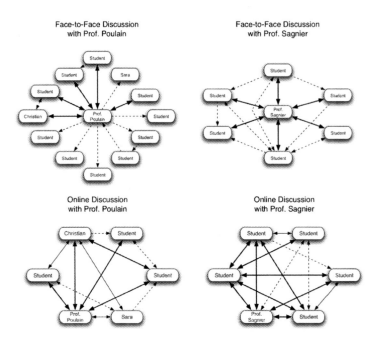

a result of the online environment, as I show in the next part of this chapter.

3.2.1.1 Prof. Sagnier

Prof. Sagnier, a native French speaker, is an excellent teacher and has the support of a large language department at a major university. The size of the department enables her to have a small class size—only six students in this study. She always has a cheerful attitude and specifically chooses open-ended topics to spur discussion. Based on the research relating to disinhibition in the foreign language classroom, Prof. Sagnier's class should be an ideal learning situation. Unfortunately, the students still do not feel comfortable talking in the classroom. When Prof. Sagnier asks a question to begin the discussion, she usually receives no response. Eventually, she must call on a specific student. In order to keep the conversation going, she finds herself forced to reply to each student comment. As a result, she is almost always the pivotal figure; the discussions are reduced to a series of one-on-one conversations involving Prof. Sagnier.

Consider the following typical classroom discussion:

(Face-to-face discussion in Prof. Sagnier's classroom)

1. **Prof. Sagnier (instructor):** And then imagine, that will be very strange. Society in one hundred years will be very curious, yes? One can imagine. So, "My professional occupation when I'm forty years old will be..." What will you do? Omar, what will you do? *(Et puis imaginez, ça va être très curieux. La societé dans cent ans sera très curieux, oui? On peut imaginer. Alors. "Mon occupation professionelle à quarante ans sera..." Qu'est-ce que vous ferez? Omar, qu'est-ce que tu feras?)*

2. **Omar:** Ummm... I don't know what occupation, but I hope that I will be happy with my occupation! *(Ummm...Je ne sais pas l'occupation mais j'espère que je vais être content avec ma profession!)*

3. **Prof. Sagnier (instructor):** Oh, but that's good! Ok.
Good idea, ok. And you, Susan? *(Ah, mais c'est bien!*
D'accord. Bonne idée, d'accord. Et toi, Susan?)
4. **Susan:** I don't have any ideas right now, but I think that
I will be in the FBI, and... *(Je n'ai pas des idées main-*
tenant mais je pense que je vais être dans le FBI, et...)
5. **Prof. Sagnier (instructor):** FBI? You want to be?
(FBI? Tu veux être?)

Not only does Prof. Sagnier comment between nearly every
student statement, her fluency in the language means that
she has significantly more to say. Students in this study
averaged 6.71 words per turn; Prof. Sagnier averaged
25.04 words per turn. The result is that she spoke 82% of
the total words, while the students combined spoke just
18% of the total.

As a result of this one-on-one pattern of interaction, students tend to direct comments to the instructor rather than
to one another. Therefore, Prof. Sagnier becomes the link
between students; in the conversations, almost all comments focus on the instructor. Figure 3 shows a graph of
this participation pattern. Each edge in the graph represents a comment specifically directed from one individual
to another. Each comment might be a question, reply, or
simply a directed comment. Dashed edges represent one to
five comments, thin black edges represent six to ten comments, and bold black edges represent more than ten comments. From this analysis, it is easy to see the degree to
which Prof. Sagnier, as the teacher, is the pivotal figure in
the classroom conversations.

Prof. Sagnier is the pivotal figure in the classroom largely because no one answers her attempts to begin discussions. When she asks a general question online, however, she frequently receives a flood of responses. Almost all students seem to participate in the conversations without prompting. As a result, she can relax control and let the conversations develop among the students. The following shows a typical portion of online conversation:

(Online conversation with Prof. Sagnier)

1. **Prof. Sagnier:** If architecture annoys you... ask me questions (not about clubs) about France. *(Si l'archi vous embête.. posez-moi des questions (pas sur les boîtes...) sur la France.)*

2. **Jean:** Where in France are you from? *(vous etes d'ou en france?)*

3. **Buzz:** France...do you know a small village named La Fleche? *(la france... connaissez-vous un toute petite ville qui s'appelle La Fleche?)*

4. **Prof. Sagnier:** Paris *(Paris.)*

5. **Buzz:** near Angers? *(près d'Angers?)*

6. **Christian:** If you want, madame, I can give them a small history of the monuments in Haiti... *(Si vous voulez, madame, je puis leur donner une petite histoire sur les monuments en Haïti...)*

7. **Buzz:** I spent 3 weeks there... it was stupid... there was NOTHING to do except learn French. *(Je passais 3 semaines là... c'était bête... il n'y a RIEN à faire sauf au'apprendre le Françasi.)*

8. **Buzz:** Paris... I love it! *(paris... j'aime bien!)*

9. **Jean:** or Vendargues, near Montpellier? I was living there in sixth grade *(ou Vendargues, pres de Montpellier? C'est la ou je suis habite en 6eme)*

10. **Blondie:** if we are not talking about architecture.... what is the subject now? *(si nous ne parlons pas sur d'archi.... quel est le sujet maintentant?)*

11. **Buzz:** There, there is TOO MUCH to do. *(Là, il y a TROP à faire.)*

12. **Prof. Sagnier:** Yes, go for the monuments of Haiti *(Oui, va pour les monuments d'Haiti)*

13. **Christian:** Do you want the historical monuments or the voodoo monuments? *(Vous voulez monuments historiques ou vaudou?)*

In the online environment, Prof. Sagnier spoke much less often, speaking only 6% of the total words. Her comments became much more equal to students comments; she averaged 7.08 words per turn while the students averaged 6.07 words per turn. Typically several students would comment between each of Prof. Sagnier's comments. Although she continued to ask both general questions and questions targeted at specific individuals, the students began replying much more to one another. In fact, whispered comments—the online equivalent of passing notes that no one else can see—were almost always written in French. From this student-to-student interaction, a much more complete graph appeared.

The first time Prof. Sagnier hosted an IRC Français-based conversation, the amount of French generated by the students surprised her. At the time, she commented on how shocked and excited she was that she could not type fast enough to insert her opinion. The students took control of the conversation, not waiting for her mediation before replying. Often, she found that the students had taken the conversations in a different direction, before she had a chance to respond. She was surprised by this, but fascinated that the mediation of an online environment seemed to draw the students out. While her experience suggests a concern about students potentially getting left behind if they cannot type fast enough, no students cited this as a problem.

3.2.1.2 Prof. Poulain

Like Prof. Sagnier, Prof. Poulain's cheerful attitude and well-chosen conversation topics make him stand out. In fact, students frequently take his courses simply on the basis that he is the teacher. Despite this, Prof. Poulain also experiences the same difficulties as Prof. Sagnier. In classroom conversations, his voice dominates; he spoke nearly 84% of the total words in the classes I examined. Like Prof. Sagnier, he feels a need to comment on each student statement, hindering student-to-student interaction. Again, this results in making him the pivotal figure in the conversation; all conversation passes through him. As he manages the conversation, he says significantly more than his students. While his students said 7.70 words each turn, he averaged 39.45 words per turn.

When hosting discussions on IRC Français, however, Prof. Poulain faced the same situation as Prof. Sagnier— students who never seemed to talk in class rapidly joined into the conversation online. In fact, the students frequently took charge of the conversation. In one discussion, Prof. Poulain's suggested topic of discussion was to compare the attitudes of Americans and the French with respect to women in the workforce. One student, however, had broken up with his girlfriend the previous evening and really wanted to talk about that experience. The other students online decided to give this individual the emotional support he needed, ignoring Prof. Poulain's topic until significantly later in the conversation. Prof. Poulain found this exciting since it met his primary goal—to engage the students in the French language.

Like Prof. Sagnier's experience, typically many students commented between each of Prof. Poulain's comments. Using IRC Français reduced his 'talking' time from 84% of the words spoken in the classroom to 14% of the words used online. Students still averaged 6.04 words per turn in these discussions, but he decreased from 39.45 words per turn to 7.58 words per turn. Again, Prof. Poulain became a more equal force in the conversations.

3.2.2 An Aside: New Social Expectations

When comparing the participation of the instructor with the participation of the students, the online environment seems to make the conversations much more equal and democratic. When comparing students, however, different levels of participation are clearly visible. In some cases, these levels of participation simply reflect personality differences among individuals. Some students are simply more gregarious than others. This personality trait comes out online as much as it would face-to-face. Individual participation differences are apparent, but even the least involved student online is more involved than the majority of students are in the classroom. Nevertheless, personality differences do not seem to completely explain participation differences.

The different set of social expectations online lead students to treat online discussions differently from how they treat classroom discussions. On the positive side, they feel freer to take control of the conversation and change the power dynamics of the situation. On the negative side, however, many students do not feel compelled to treat the online conversations with the same respect that they have for classroom conversations. Commonly, students who initially seem to have had limited participation in an online conversation were simply not present for much of that conversation. Frequently, students arrive at the online conversations late or leave the discussion early. Late arrival means that either that newcomers must struggle to join the conversation-in-progress, or that someone must review the conversation in order to bring the newcomer up to speed. Leaving early leaves a conversational gap that had previously been filled. Dealing with this gap often slows discussion, as the remaining interlocutors must, in essence, regroup. I return to these themes in the next chapter when I examine the impact of these behavioral changes on the quality of the content of the discussion.

3.3 EXPLAINING BEHAVIORAL CHANGES

It is not enough to simply know that these behavioral changes occur when conversations move from the classroom to the chatroom. In order to be able to design better online learning environments, we must ask why these changes occur. How is the medium influencing the levels of disinhibition that we observe? In Chapter 2, I briefly described several theories of disinhibition in online environments, all with some degree of explanatory power. In this chapter, I provide a new way of looking at this problem that (1) draws together aspects of these theories of disinhibition and (2) provides a new way of thinking through the design issues that might be applicable to more than chat environments. In particular, I draw on the bystander effect—a social psychological theory that attempted to explain inhibition in emergency settings—to provide a framework for looking at how design decisions can influence inhibition in the classroom and in the chatroom.

Note that social psychology's understanding of individual motivation in group settings, which is now typically referred to as *social loafing* research[11] (e.g., Karau & Williams, 1993), has progressed significantly since the bystander effect was first studied in the late 1960s. Because researchers looking at the bystander effect asked a different set of questions from today's social loafing researchers, it makes sense to return to this older research. Today, social loafing researchers focus on understanding how features of the social and physical environment influence the level of motivation that individuals feel for group tasks. In contrast, research into the bystander effect examined at how group settings inhibit individuals from taking actions. Although motivation and inhibition are clearly related, they seem to have different underlying social psychological mechanisms. In this section, I set aside motivations, which have been studied extensively in educational settings (e.g., Pintrich & Schunk, 1996), in order to ask questions about inhibitions.

In the next section, I provide some background on the bystander effect as a social psychological phenomenon, before showing how it can be used as a lens for examining educational environments.

3.3.1 The Bystander Effect: A Lens
for Understanding Participation

In 1964, the story surrounding Kitty Genovese's murder was sufficiently shocking for it to warrant national media coverage. As Genovese returned to her New York City apartment one evening, she was followed by a stranger. In a stairwell plainly visible from other apartments, this stranger attacked her. During the next half hour, thirty-eight of her neighbors heard her screams and witnessed her murder from their windows, but none so much as called the police,[12] much less intervened (Rosenthal, 1964/1999). It would be nice to believe that this failure to help was an isolated incident, but less extreme examples happen every day. Just consider, for example, the number of people who never think of stopping to help when driving by someone on the side of the road struggling with a flat tire. Although a number of explanations for non-response—e.g., apathy, habituation, and fear of reprisal—can legitimately be posited in any of these emergencies, the unifying theme ultimately seems to lie in the social psychological phenomenon termed the bystander effect (Latané & Darley, 1970).

Essentially, the bystander effect suggests that individuals are less likely to offer assistance in an emergency when other witnesses are around. It is not that people are primarily apathetic or that they fear reprisal; rather, the presence of a group actively inhibits individuals from acting in an emergency situation. The bystander effect itself is not a psychological mechanism. Rather, it is convenient shorthand to refer to a number of related mechanisms that will be discussed below.

A number of studies by Bibb Latané, John Darley, and their students offer evidence for this effect.[13] For example, one study examined how people react to ambiguous, but potentially dangerous situations (Latané & Darley, 1968). In this study, the subjects were male college students who believed that they were waiting to be interviewed about the problems of urban life. While the subject was filling out the preliminary forms, the room began to fill with acrid smoke. When the student waited alone, he generally reported the smoke calmly almost as soon as he noticed it. When the subject waited with two confederates[14] who were trained not to respond to the smoke, only 10% reported the problem before the designated six minute stopping point. Surprisingly, however, when the subject waited with two other naïve subjects, response rates were still low. In other words, when all three subjects were completely free to respond, the presence of others actively inhibited each individual from taking action. Latané and Darley (1968) suggest that the reason this happens is that each individual attempts to determine the potential danger present in the situation simultaneously. In part, each individual does this by consciously or unconsciously examining how the others interpret the situation. Each, then, interprets the others' reactions as calm rather than as confusion. Therefore, individual attempts to disambiguate the situation serve as social cues that inhibit the behaviors of others.

In another study, Latané and Rodin (1969) examined a situation where there was less ambiguity. Male college students were recruited to participate in market research relating to board games. After showing the subject to a waiting room, the female interviewer crossed through a curtain to work while the subject filled out a preliminary questionnaire. While the subject worked, he heard the sound of a crashing cabinet and the interviewer calling out in pain that her ankle was hurt and that she couldn't move. When subjects were alone, they immediately attempted to help nearly 70% of the time. When subjects waited with a passive confederate—one trained not to respond—the response rate dropped to less than 10%. Like the previous study, subjects waiting with another naïve subject responded more than with the passive confederate, but significantly less than when alone. Even when subjects waited with friends, they still showed significant signs of inhibition.

Through these and other studies (e.g., Darley & Latané, 1968; Latané & Darley, 1969), Latané and Darley (1970) built a model of the decisions that must be made before a bystander will intervene in an emergency. First, the bystander needs to notice the emergency. Then, the bystander needs to interpret the situation as one in which action by someone is necessary. Once the bystander interprets the situation as an emergency, he or she must further interpret it as one in which he or she specifically should act. Next, the bystander needs to determine what form the action should take. Finally, he or she must act. At any point in this decision tree, the bystander can cycle back to previous decision points; it is not a linear decision process. Decisions can become blocked when one stage of the decision tree cannot be decided upon. In these cases, bystanders will often exhibit signs of extreme discomfort over inaction. Delayed response will often lead to inaction altogether. The longer a bystander waits to respond, the less likely he or she is to ever actually respond.

When an individual is alone and is presented with an emergency or situation requiring assistance, he or she is likely to help (Latané, 1970). When other people are present, however, any given individual is significantly less likely to help. The likelihood of the emergency victim receiving any help at all decreases as the number of bystanders increases (Latané & Darley, 1968). Four mechanisms contribute to this phenomenon (Latané & Darley, 1970):

- **Self-awareness:**[15] The (perceived) presence of an audience inhibits individuals from acting. No one wants to appear foolish or inappropriate in front of others.
- **Social cues:** Individuals actively look to one another for cues about how to behave in the situation. The inaction of others will likely cause the inaction of the individual. These social cues can interact with the other mechanisms to increase the effect.

- **Blocking:** It is often the case that multiple bystanders taking action can make the emergency worse. The action—or perceived/suspected action—of one bystander effectively blocks others from taking action.

- **Diffuse responsibility:** In a situation where only a small percentage of the bystanders can take action, responsibility is diffuse. Each individual feels only limited responsibility for the negative consequences of inaction.

The interaction between these four mechanisms is complex, but dealing with them separately provides a way to observe significant and salient behavior in both emergency and non-emergency situations. This allows us to begin asking questions about the interaction of these mechanisms with one another.

Although the bystander effect specifically refers to emergency situations, there is reason to believe that it can also help explain differences between classroom and online behavior. This is not to say that classrooms experience "the bystander effect" per se. Classrooms and emergency situations are quite different environments. However, similarities in social behavior in the two situations often emerge because they are influenced by similar underlying social and psychological phenomena. I claim that similarities and differences in phenomena observed between emergency situations and classrooms may be caused by similarities and differences in those underlying phenomena, as I shall explore in detail. The bystander effect is a pattern of social behavior that typically emerges in situations with certain key characteristics. This regularity of behavior across different emergency situations is caused by underlying social and psychological phenomena. It is important not to reify the notion of the bystander effect; it is an observed pattern, not a causal entity. A well-understood pattern is a lens that can help make sense of future observations, in situations that are both like and unlike the original situation. From this pattern of social interaction, we can begin asking questions to inform the design of new educational environments.

In the next section, I present a case study of differing participation patterns between a face-to-face environment and IRC Français. Through this case study, I show how the mechanisms of the bystander effect help structure observations about some of the underlying causes for these differences. In doing so, I do not suggest that the bystander effect provides all of the answers. Rather, it serves as a lens through which some of the possible answers become evident. Further research is needed to explore how these mechanisms play out in other technological media.

3.3.2 Case Study: Participation in IRC Français

Earlier, I showed how conversations in a classroom and conversations in an online chatroom exhibit different interaction patterns. In the classroom, students rarely respond to the teacher's questions without being explicitly called upon. As such, the instructor becomes a pivotal figure who controls the flow of the conversation. Online, however, students respond to the teacher's questions. The conversation becomes more of a group discussion than a series of one-on-one interactions. To understand why students seem to participate differently when they enter an online environment, I focus here on a case study of two particular students from Prof. Poulain's classroom. Christian was a vocal, confident student whose behavior changed little when conversations took place online. Sara, on the other hand, was a quiet, shy student in the classroom but one who participated much more actively in the online environment. Examining these two students illustrates how the bystander effect can help us understand their behavioral changes.

Sara was a shy freshman who took this class in her second semester at Georgia Tech. She described her first reaction to the class as:

> I don't really talk that much in French class because the first day I came in, I heard everyone else speaking and realized that they had all been to France and they were very good at it.

In a class of twelve students, Sara was one of three freshmen. She had two and a half years of French education in high school and one semester in college. She was intimidated by the others in the room and their variety of experiences with the French language. As she indicated on the introductory survey:

> Because I am unable to speak very fluently, I dread the conversational portion of learning French.

Christian was the opposite. Although Sara was a shy freshman, Christian was a confident senior. Born in Haiti, a

French-speaking country, Christian immigrated to the United States with his immediate family at approximately the same time that he began his studies at Georgia Tech. In Haiti, he was raised by a relatively wealthy family in this poor country. Having moved to the United States, Christian has a strong desire to be able to share some of his experiences in Haiti with his classmates, whom he views as sheltered:

> Ever since I had a French class here, I've wanted to have a sit down with the students and tell them, for me, as in the upper-middle class in Haiti, how hard it was even though you have money. Meaning how worthless money was because it was just the country that was unbearable. I wanted them to ask me questions. I wanted to tell them what it feels like to see dead bodies in the street, or cut up bodies in the street, or have TVs with no censorship showing, like, burnt body parts. These things are things you never think about when you are in the States.

He sometimes seems slightly arrogant or condescending, but this particular desire to expose the other students to his experiences in Haiti doesn't come across that way. Rather, it comes across as a need to cope with a deeply personal tragedy through sharing with others. With a smile, he describes why he is often more talkative than others in a classroom:

> The more personal [it] get[s], the more you talk.
> I guess that's why I talk a lot. I take everything personally.

Clearly the best French speaker in the class, Christian often dominates the discussion.

In the classroom, Prof. Poulain uses many common pedagogical practices for increasing student engagement, but with only limited success. He arranges the room in a circle so that all students can see one another. He often uses a text—e.g., a book chapter, a newspaper article— as the starting point for classroom discussions, so that all students have some foundation from which to participate. He tries to supplement the more academic reading material with interesting personal or cultural stories and anecdotes:

> I usually try to challenge them by assuming or stating things that might not necessarily be true that I know will get a reaction. ... [In the classroom, I try to have students] compare what you're learning to what you know and how they can relate.

Although many students seem to actively listen, few actually join the discussion. Sara and Christian represent the extremes that are seen in the class. In the classroom conversations that I observed, the only time that Sara spoke was when explicitly called upon to read from the text. Periodically, Prof. Poulain had all students work in pairs in order to require all students to participate. In these cases, Sara interacted with her partner, but required her interlocutor to present their discussion to the class.

Christian, on the other hand, was extremely vocal. In fact, often Prof. Poulain would attempt to explicitly ignore him so that other students would have a chance to interact as well. Just as often, Christian would attempt to assist

Prof. Poulain when he struggled for the right phrase, or would introduce obscure French cultural references into the discussion in order to show off his knowledge. In one particular example, Prof. Poulain had commented on how a particular phrase tended to be a tongue twister for American students. This led into Prof. Poulain providing a common French tongue twister for the class to attempt. Rather than moving on, however, Christian insisted on offering examples that he knew, even though Prof. Poulain's tone and body language strongly suggested that he would rather take the discussion in different directions:

(Classroom Discussion)

1. **Prof. Poulain:** Yes, yes. They exist, for example, we have things like "Ces cypress sont si loin qu'on ne sait si s'en sont." *(Oui, oui. ça existe, par exemple on a des choses comme, "Ces cypres sont si loin qu'on ne sait si s'en sont.")*

2. (A few students talk at once.)

3. **Prof. Poulain:** Yes, "les chaussettes de l'archi du chesse..." We say that, it is a more literary term, it is alliteration. *(Oui, "les chaussettes de l'archi du chesse..." On dit ca, c'est le terme plus literaire, c'est des alliterations.)*

4. **Christian:** Tongue twister *("Les poissons sont boissons en poison.")*

5. **Prof. Poulain:** Yes, things like that. (Oui, des trucs comme ca.)

6. **Christian:** Tongue twister *("Les deux minutes de minuit diminus.")*

7. **Prof. Poulain:** Ok, not bad. Ok, I'm going to write some to see if you know them. "Ces cypress sont si loin qu'on ne sait si s'en sont." *(Ok, pas mal. D'accord on va ecrire quelques-uns pour voir si vous les connaisses. "Ces cypres sont si loin qu'on ne sait si s'en sont.")*

Although Christian and Sara represent the extremes of the students in the classroom, few approached Christian's lack of inhibition. Rather, most waited to be called on before participating. In looking at the classroom, Prof. Poulain was almost always the pivotal figure. Nearly all of the students' comments were directed to him. Although Prof. Poulain managed to maintain a dialog with the students for the class period, discussion between students rarely occurred unless Prof. Poulain divided them into small groups for exercises.

When online, however, things were rather different. Consider the following online conversation that occurred relatively early in the semester. This segment takes place immediately after Sara enters the chatroom several minutes late. Before she entered, the others had been discussing various differences between major world cultures:

(Online Discussion)

1. **Prof. Poulain:** welcome Sara *(bienvenu Sara)*
2. **Christian:** good day sara *(bonjour sara)*
3. **Anne:** hello sara *(salut sara)*
4. **Sara:** hello everyone *(salut tout le monde)*
5. **Christian:** well, now we are five! *(alors nous sommes cinq!)*

6. **Prof. Poulain:** Yes, it is better than 4 *(Oui, c'est mieux que 4)*

7. **Christian:** lol *(lol)*

8. **Anne:** Yes, it is good today! *(Oui, c'est bon aujourd hui!)*

9. **Prof. Poulain:** Do you know some things about work in France that you would like to share? *(Vous savez des choses sur le travail en France que vous voulez partager?)*

10. **Christian:** hmmm *(hmmm)*

11. **Anne:** I know nothing about work in France... *(Je ne sais rien du travail en France...)*

12. **Christian:** how much time is necessary to have a job as *(combien de temps faut-il pour avoir un travail comme)*

13. **Prof. Poulain:** There are many news articles about the 35-hour work week for everyone *(Il ya beaucoup de nouvelles sur la semaine de 35 heures pour tout le monde)*

14. **Christian:** a lawyer or a doctor *(avocat, ou medecin)*

15. **Christian:** how much time in school *(combien de temps a l'ecole)*

16. **Prof. Poulain:** One needs to study about ten year after the BAC to be a doctor, it's a little less for a lawyer *(Il faut etudier une dizaine d'annee apres le BAC pour etre medecin, c'est un peu moins long pour etre avocet)*

17. **Prof. Poulain:** years *(d'aannees)*

18. **Prof. Poulain:** How many hours per week do you work Anne? *(Combien d'heure par semaine travailles-tu Anne?)*

19. **Sara:** I have a question... Who wants a 35-hour week? *(J'ai une question... Qui veut la semaine de 35 heures?)*

20. **Anne:** Ten years after the bac??? *(Une dizaine après le bac???)*
21. **Christian:** it takes a lot of time to travel to work, doesn't it *(il faut beaucoup de temps pour voyager au travail, n'est-ce pas)*
22. **Prof. Poulain:** If you want to specialize... less time to be a generalist! *(Si on veut se specialiser... moins longtemps pour etre generaliste!)*
23. **Sara:** I know that in the United States, people who work want to work more hours to earn more money... *(Je sais qu'aux Etats-Unis, les gens qui travaillent veulent travailler beaucoup d'heures pour gagner plus d'argent...)*
24. **Prof. Poulain:** It depends on where one lives, in the Paris region yes *(Ca depend ou on habite, dans la region parisienne oui)*
25. **Prof. Poulain:** the 35-hour week argument means that people are not allowed to work more than 35 hours *(la semaine de 35 heures veut dire que personne n'est authorise a travailler + de 35 heures)*
26. **Prof. Poulain:** Right now, there is a 40-hour week for most places *(Pour l'instant, il y a la semaine de 40 heures dans beaucoup d'endroits)*
27. **Christian:** how does one say "salary" *(comment dit-on "salary")*
28. **Christian:** "des appointements?" *(des appointements?)*
29. **Prof. Poulain:** salary is "le salaire" – Do you think we should limit the number of work hours? *(salary is le salaire—Est-ce que vous pensez qu'on devrait limiter le nombre d'heures de travail?)*

30. **Prof. Poulain:** salary or disappointment? *(appointment ou desappointment?)*

31. **Christian:** I don't know, but it's good for people who earn a salary - less work and the same salary? *(je ne sais pas, mais c'est bon pour les gens qui gagne un salaire - moins de travail et le même salaire?)*

32. **Christian:** money *(gagnent)*

33. *Sara:* I think it is the individual's choice how many hours he works... *(Je pense que c'est le choix d'individuel combien d'heures il travail...)*

34. **Prof. Poulain:** The workers want to be able to work more sometimes, the businesses must hire more people as well (to hire) *(Les travailleurs veulent pouvoir travailler + parfois, les entreprises doivent embaucher + de personnes aussi (to hire)*

35. **Sara:** But if one wants a good job with a large salary, he must work a lot of hours *(Mais si on veut un bon job avec un grand salaire, il doit travailler beaucoup d'heures)*

36. **Prof. Poulain:** It's true that the individual's choice is not always the choice that makes the state or the country! *(C'est vrai le choix de l'individu n'est pas toujours le choix que fait l'etat ou le pays!)*

37. **Christian:** not if one can work only 35 hours per week *(pas si on ne peut travailler que 35 pour semaine)*

38. **Prof. Poulain:** Of course, the CEOs are not included in the 35-hour week, they are not paid by the hour, but by the month! *(Bien sur les CEO ne sont pas inclus dans la semaines*

```
        de 35 heures, il ne sont pas paye a l'heure
        mais au mois!)
39.  Christian: oh (oh)
40.  Christian: I see (je vois)
```

Notice a number of interesting things that happen in this segment. First, the greetings do not resemble the typical greetings in a classroom. Should a student arrive late in a small class, it is common to hear the instructor greet the student, but it is uncommon to hear the others greet the student. It is equally uncommon for the student to verbally respond. For better or for worse, arriving late is more socially acceptable online than in a traditional classroom. Face to face, a late arrival is disruptive. Online, not only can the classroom conversation proceed uninterrupted, but teacher and classmates can also greet the student individually. This small detail contributes to creating a warm, welcoming atmosphere. I will discuss this type of conversational tangent in further detail in the section on blocking below.

Next, Prof. Poulain introduces the concept of the workweek, particularly in France. After waiting a few minutes to determine what was going on in the environment, Sara jumps in with a question, "I have a question… Who wants a 35-hour week? *(J'ai une question… Qui veut la semaine de 35 heures?)*" It is interesting to note Sara actively participating in the conversation. This is different from her behavior in the classroom. Not only is she actively participating, she is also explicitly questioning the assumptions of the Professor's previous statement. When in the classroom, she is the shy student who hides away. In the online environment, she is an active interlocutor who (respectfully) engages the professor as peer.

3.4 DISCUSSION

In this particular case study, behavioral changes clearly occur when discussions move from the classroom to the online environment. Why do these particular changes happen? Why isn't Christian affected in the same way as Sara? Are these changes doing anything to improve the learning experience? In this section, I explore evidence for learning in these online discussions before turning to the underlying psychological mechanisms.

3.4.1 Learning

Before exploring the mechanisms behind these behavioral changes, I need to examine whether or not there is evidence that these changes might be educationally beneficial. Although I did not conduct formal evaluations of learning, student comments suggest that they did learn through the online conversations. For example, Sara's discussion of her learning through IRC Français reflected the comments of many of the other students interviewed:

> If I ever go to France, I think that through this [experience on IRC Français], I could carry on a good conversation with someone and feel comfortable with what I know and what I'm saying. ... I think a lot of it was review for me. I had seen everything before. It was just a

matter of putting it together. We had not done
a lot of that because most of my classes were
standard textbook and you didn't really have
to think on the spot. So, I think a lot of what I
learned was putting things together and having
it make sense.

In her previous language learning experience, Sara was
exposed to a number of concepts that are necessary for
speaking a foreign language. The textbooks that provided
the foundation for these courses, however, tended to treat
each concept as a separate unit. Like novice physicists who
structure problems in fragmentary ways (Chi, Feltovich, &
Glaser, 1981), Sara's knowledge of the French language at
the beginning of class was also largely fragmented into a
variety of "problem types" or grammatical structures. The
conversational practice that she experienced in IRC Français
provided her with opportunities to begin integrating this
knowledge in a meaningful and flexible way.

The conversations on IRC Français also gave Sara the
opportunity to begin developing more fluent recall:

It's like once you pick up on it and get used to
it—at first, I was really, really bad trying to keep
up and trying to think of what I was going to say,
but towards the end, as I said, I was thinking in
French and I didn't have to think in English and
translate into French. I think that was a great help
and I do believe that I'm going to remember a lot
of that portion of it—like just having the words
and phrases click in my mind. I think that's going
to be the most important part rather than remem-
bering specific words or specific phrases.

At other times in the interview, Sara spoke about the interactive nature of the online discussions and how that helped her learn to play with the French language to get out of binds where she did not know the exact words to convey her thoughts. She spoke of learning to rephrase her thoughts in order to convey her meaning, even if she did not know the exact words. In other words, she felt that she learned how to adapt the vocabulary and grammar to suit new situations.

The strongest critique of this type of online environment, however, is that it doesn't offer much time or support for reflection—an important component of learning (e.g., Schön, 1987; Kolodner, 1997). As I discuss below, the lack of blocking allows for some greater reflection as students compose their comments, but the environment alone seems to offer limited further reflection. In a rapid, synchronous conversation, the student who takes time to reflect conscientiously on various statements will be quickly left behind. Not only does the medium itself discourage reflection, but reduced inhibition/self-awareness also has been shown to correlate with reduced reflection (Greenberg & Pyszczynski, 1986). Reflection, however, should not necessarily occur at the time that an activity is carried out. Rather, it can be appropriately conducted after the fact. Thus, although text does rapidly scroll off the screen in a chat environment, saving the text for later reflection poses no challenge.

Recognizing the problems of reflection, one teacher regularly using IRC Français with her classes specifically used the transcripts in the classroom as an anchor for further conversations. After her class met online, she reviewed the transcripts to determine common errors. During the next class session, she based grammatical lessons on the common errors she identified. As homework, she expected her students to go through their own transcripts and correct a small handful of their own errors. In this way, she was able to get feedback regarding her students' progress and encourage students to reflect on their own mistakes and those of their peers. At the same time, however, students never had to correct all of their mistakes. She reports that her students responded enthusiastically to this type of learning activity.

Since there is reason to believe that this type of online environment contributes to foreign language learning, understanding the behavioral changes observed may help us better understand learning in other online environments. In the next section, I use the features of the bystander effect—self-awareness, social cues, diffuse responsibility, and blocking—to structure this case study. I show how self-awareness seems to be reduced in the online environment, facilitated by changes in social cues and blocking mechanisms. I also show how diffuse responsibility appears to play a role in both environments, but does not explain the behavioral differences observed.

3.4.2 Self-Awareness
There is evidence that changes in self-awareness contribute to the behavioral differences seen between these particular

environments. Recall that self-awareness is an individual's conscious awareness of others making judgments about that individual (Duval & Wicklund, 1972; Silvia & Duval, 2001). It says nothing about whether or not others actually make such judgments; rather, it refers to the perception of the individual. A person with a high level of self-awareness is highly conscious of others judging him or her, regardless of whether anyone is actually doing so. Self-awareness, however, does not directly influence how well students perform in a given environment; rather, the level of confidence with which a student enters the situation moderates the influence of self-awareness on performance. Zajonc (1965) found that increased self-awareness helped highly confident students perform better, while it lowered the performance of low confidence students. Likewise, lowered self-awareness helps improve the performance of low-confidence students, while degrading the performance of high-confidence students. With Sara and Christian, we see evidence of this relationship between self-awareness (moderated by confidence) and conversational participation.

The differing confidence between Sara and Christian can be seen clearly in how they interact in the classroom. For example, Christian often responds to Prof. Poulain's general questions without raising his hand. He is comfortable interacting with others in French because his language abilities are significantly greater than the other students in the class. Growing up in Haiti, he had significant exposure to the language and probably should be in a more advanced class. He is rightfully confident that his abilities are better than the other students in the class. Christian describes himself as "fluent in French" and often talks about enjoying "being able to help [the other students] improve their skills."

Sara, however, does not have nearly the same abilities or confidence as Christian. Her abilities are much more comparable to the others in the classroom, and she has not had the experience of being immersed in a French-speaking culture. She judges the other students to be better at speaking the language, which causes her to participate less. Sara lacks confidence in her language abilities in part because she judges them to be worse than the other students in the class.

Although Sara and Christian have different levels of confidence in the classroom, they both seem to experience increased self-awareness. Christian expressed the general awareness that students have of an audience when they are in the classroom:

> In class when you are being asked a question and you have to say something, you become very hesitant. And then you're wondering whether you're saying the right thing or not, whether the teacher is going to say something. ... I've noticed that a lot of people in my class lack the confidence. They don't believe that their French is actually good.

In the classroom, students are strongly aware of an audience making judgments of their actions; self-awareness increases in the classroom. Christian continued to contrast the classroom with the online environment:

> [Online] they feel they are able to express their
> opinion or say something without really feeling
> the burden of eyes around them or feeling that
> they said something that wasn't too correct.

In the online environment, students do not feel the same sense of a judging audience; self-awareness is significantly lower online (e.g., Matheson & Zanna, 1988).

According to Zajonc's social facilitation theory, we should expect that the high confidence students perform better with higher self-awareness and that the low confidence students perform better with lower self-awareness, as shown in Table 1. In the case of learning conversational skills in a foreign language, performance is largely intertwined with participation. Therefore, we should expect to see participation relate to confidence and self-awareness. This is certainly the case with Sara's performance in these environments. As

Table 1. The Interaction Between Confidence
and Self-Awareness

	High Self-Awareness (face-to-face)	Low Self-Awareness (online)
High Confidence (Christian)	Increased performance and participation	Decreased performance and participation
Low Confidence (Sara)	Decreased performance and participation	Increased performance and participation

discussed above, she says almost nothing in the classroom, but takes a more active role in conversations online:

> I liked it. I spoke much more. ... I got to know my French class really well at the end and I started thinking in French.

She speaks of how the online experience helped her begin to develop the confidence to speak in face-to-face settings:

> I also found that I knew more French than I gave myself credit for. ... I'm not scared to speak French now. When I see some of the people outside of class, I'll say something in French to them. The friendships that were built through the chatroom has given me the confidence to speak more.

Reduced self-awareness in the online environment seemed to interact with Sara's low confidence, and helped her to participate more. In doing so, she found that her abilities were good enough to give her the increased confidence to participate more in face-to-face environments where self-awareness is significantly greater. In the case of Christian, we see relatively little change in his participation patterns. He speaks a lot in the classroom and he speaks a lot online.

Christian is generally confident in his language abilities and performs well no matter which environment he is in. Sara, however, has little confidence, but performs better in the online environment than she does in the classroom. This suggests that much of the participation change stems from a reduction in self-awareness in the online environment. Why is self-awareness reduced online? As I discuss in the next sections, part of it comes from the absence of certain social cues and from non-blocking interaction.

3.4.3 Social Cues

Some of the behavioral differences observed in the online environment likely stem from the reduced social cues available, but not in the ways that we might expect. Previous literature on the reduction of social cues in online environments, suggests that people are generally less inhibited online because they do not have to endure the disapproving looks of others when they violate social norms (e.g., Weisband, 1992). Comments by Sara and Christian, however, indicate that this is less of a concern than we would expect. Rather, students seem to worry that others can pick up on mistakes easier in the classroom because they can see the extra social cues (stuttering, long pauses, etc.) that highlight the mistake.

As Christian said, students can interact online "without really feeling the burden of eyes around them." Sara, however, pointed out that the fear of others staring at her does not relate to judgmental looks or any other social cues from the other students. Rather, she is aware that she has small signs, like a player's tell in a game of poker, that give away when she has made a mistake:

> If I mess up in class, I kind of look around or
> I pause. No one can notice that online. I don't

stutter online if I mess up on a word. I don't have long pauses online. ... I didn't really talk [in the classroom] because I didn't want them to hear me mess up, but on the French chatroom, it was easier to talk because I had my French-English dictionary right there and I could pick up on what other people were saying easier.

Sara is concerned that others in the classroom can see cues—stuttering, pausing, consulting the dictionary—that indicate that she's made a mistake. Talking online allows Sara to have a space where her tells are not so visible. Although this stems from a reduction in social cues, it is interesting to note that it has to do with the social cues of the individual making mistakes rather than those of the others observing that individual.

3.4.4 Blocking

In most face-to-face settings such as the classroom, blocking often plays a prominent role. In polite conversation, only one person can speak at once. If one person has the conversational floor, all others are effectively blocked from actively participating (Wennerstrom & Siegel, 2003). When conversations take place online, however, this type of blocking is removed (Cherny, 1999). If one person is typing or composing a response, all others are also free to do so. One person's participation cannot block another from participating. Because of the nature of the medium, students interacting on IRC Français experience significantly less blocking than in the classroom. This seems to contribute to the behavioral changes in two ways: (1) it provides students with a space to reflect on their comments before making them public and (2) it actively hinders the initiate-respond-evaluate (IRE) cycle from forming.

When a student using IRC Français goes to add a comment to the conversation, he or she must first type out the comment, and then press "Enter." Seeing the comment in completed, written form, allows students to reflect on their comment—and make corrections—before making it publicly available. Sara commented on how this contributed to helping her feel more comfortable speaking in the online environment: "I don't have long pauses online because they can't see that I'm in the middle of typing something. That just made me feel more comfortable." Many other students echoed this theme that the online environment provided them with more time than the classroom did to think about their answers, but that this thinking time was limited by conversational norms of continuity.

Although the time to think and reflect was important for the students' comfort, lack of blocking played another role in altering the conversational norms. Lack of blocking meant that it was difficult for anyone to become a pivotal figure online. Since lack of blocking essentially allows multiple people to compose messages simultaneously, it is difficult for the instructor or anyone else to control the conversational floor. In the classroom, for example, Prof. Poulain often ignored Christian's raised hand since he was blocking the other students from participating. In the online environment, however, there is no evidence that Prof. Poulain treated Christian's input any differently than he did that of the other students. Christian was not able to block others during the discussions on IRC Français. Likewise, Prof. Poulain could not unintentionally block the students from participating. Therefore, when he was responding to someone's comment online, the discussion continued, effectively prohibiting the initiate-respond-evaluate (IRE) cycle from forming.

These changes in conversational structure seemed to allow an interesting pattern of dynamic grouping to develop. In the online conversations, small group discussions easily formed and rejoined in ways that would be impossible in a classroom setting. In the classroom, all individuals must engage in the same conversation, since only one person can talk at any given time. If a subset of the class wanted to follow up on a thread of conversation while the rest of the class continued on a different thread, they would need to physically separate and form a small group over in the corner. Of course, this is frowned upon without the instructor's explicit permission! Online, however, multiple conversations can occur simultaneously in the same chatroom. Sara described one specific example from her experiences:

> [This one time], me, Andrew, and Melissa [the other freshmen] split up and we were talking about different phrases in French and how they related to slang in American—in English—and the other people were talking about French music we had in class. I think our conversation stemmed off of that because of one of the lines in one of the songs. In the end, we rejoined, but

> for a while, we split off. It was good because it
> kept everyone involved. Everyone was talking
> to at least someone. They were on related sub-
> jects; we just went off on a tangent. It worked
> out really well, though.

In the online environment, new conversations can seam-
lessly spawn, but they can also easily reintegrate since
members of both smaller conversations remain aware of
the other group's discussion. The interleaving of comments in the online environment allows for monitoring of
peripheral conversations with reduced cognitive resources
(compared with monitoring another small group discussion
in a face-to-face, classroom setting).

3.4.5 Diffuse Responsibility

The final aspect of the bystander effect, diffuse responsibility, seems to play an important, but unchanging, role in
both the online and the classroom environment. Although
both environments exhibit evidence of diffuse responsibility, it does not help explain the behavioral differences
observed. In the classroom, when Prof. Poulain asks a question, it is unclear who should respond. As a result, often no
one responds until Prof. Poulain calls on a specific individual. As the primary exception to this rule, recall Christian's description of why he talks in class, "I guess that's
why I talk a lot. I take everything personally." Christian is
not constrained to the same type of diffuse responsibility,
because his personality naturally assumes responsibility
for answering Prof. Poulain's questions.

In the interaction on IRC Français, there is no reason to expect that diffusion of responsibility should be different, nor is there any evidence to suggest that it is. Nothing about Prof. Poulain's questions in the online environment suggests a different responsibility structure than the classroom. IRC Français allows all users to know how many others are involved in the conversation. This means that students have the same indication of others' availability to answer the teacher's questions. Diffuse responsibility seems to work similarly in both of these environments. Therefore, the behavioral changes observed suggest that the other aspects of the bystander effect play a much stronger role in this particular case than diffuse responsibility.

3.5 ALTERNATIVE INTERPRETATIONS

In using the bystander effect as a lens to explain some of the causes of participation patterns in face-to-face and chat environments, I have argued that students become more or less inhibited as a result of a complex interaction between several structural features of the educational setting. Both pedagogy and the socio-technical infrastructure influence the level of fear and inhibition that students face in speaking. Through the mechanisms of the bystander effect, I have suggested one way of breaking down these complex interactions. However, there are other potential explanations for the changing communication patterns.

One alternative interpretation holds that fear of making mistakes is generally reduced in the online environment.

This occurs through both the mechanisms I described above (i.e., social cues, self-awareness, social facilitation) and others found in the social psychology literature (i.e., social conformity [(Asch, 1951, 1956), cognitive dissonance (Festinger, 1957)], etc.). Reduced fears occur through a number of mechanisms that play a primary role in participation patterns observed.

Another explanation holds that the unique affordances of working in a textual medium allow for greater disinhibition in online environments. According to this perspective, students feel more comfortable online because they are able to take time to check their grammar or spelling before making a public statement. This explanation incorporates the benefits of removing blocking, but suggests that the other primary mechanisms at play are in giving students the ability to better control self-presentation.

These three explanations—the bystander effect, fear reduction, and affordances of text—are not mutually exclusive. It is possible that different aspects of these explanations are more important in some environments than in others. Although the bystander effect draws on previous explanations of disinhibition (c.f., Joinson, 2003), I have not attempted to present a fully formed psychological theory of behavior online. Rather, I have presented a useful lens for observing online behavior, which can help us think through the potential implications of design decisions when developing new online learning environments. More research needs to be conducted into the mechanisms underlying participation patterns, so that we may begin distinguishing between these various alternative explanations.

3.6 SUMMARY

> This is what I do not like. When we talk on the computer, everyone speaks together, but when we are in class, no one says anything. It is like we become strangers again if we are not protected by the computer. *(C'est ce que je n'aime pas. Quand on parle sur l'ordinateur, tout le monde bavard ensemble, mais quand nous sommes en classe, personne ne dit rien. C'est comme on devient des etrangeres encore si on n'est pas protege par l'ordinateur.)*
> – Student Comment on IRC Français

In foreign language learning, moving a conversation from the classroom to an online chat environment changes participation patterns (Beauvois, 1992b; Kelm, 1992; Bruce, Peyton, & Batson, 1993; Beauvois, 1994/1995; Kern, 1995; Beauvois & Eledge, 1995/1996; Beauvois, 1997; Warschauer, 1997; Hudson & Bruckman, 2002). Students feel "protected by the computer." They are more willing to speak and claim agency over the direction of discussion.[16]

Borrowing the notion of the bystander effect from social psychology provides us with a new way for influencing participation patterns in educational settings. In particular, it suggests four important sets of questions to ask in designing a new learning environment:

1. **Self-Awareness:** How much self-awareness will be promoted in the new environment? Since self-awareness interacts with confidence to affect performance, how will different students perform? Is the level of self-awareness appropriate for the anticipated level of confidence?

2. **Social Cues:** What are the social cues available in the environment? Are they likely to generate a positive feedback loop (encouraging discussion) or a negative feedback loop (discouraging discussion)? If a positive feedback loop occurs, are there features in the environment to ensure educationally productive discussions?

3. **Blocking:** Are there ways for students to block one another from participating in the environment? Can students participate in parallel, or must all students pause while one participates? Will one student's answer to a question discourage others from also commenting?

4. **Diffuse Responsibility:** How are notions of responsibility and accountability conveyed to the students in the environment?

The four mechanisms involved in the bystander effect—self-awareness, social cues, blocking, and diffuse responsibility—can help us to understand observed behavioral patterns and leverage this knowledge in the design of new systems. Not all of these mechanisms are relevant to all social settings; they simply describe common patterns of behavior. The bystander effect provides a lens onto these patterns that can help us understand complex social interaction. The question that remains, however, is: how do these behavioral changes influence the intellectual content of these discussions? In the next chapter, I focus on this question.

CHAPTER 4

INTERACTION QUALITY: A QUASI-EXPERIMENTAL STUDY

4.1 STUDYING "QUALITY"

In the last chapter, I explored why conversations in online chat environments tend to have more equitable participation than similar discussions in the classroom. In the foreign language learning domain, instructors cared more about the process of the discussion (i.e., how much students used their foreign language) than they did about the content of the discussion. The purpose of this analysis, however, is to help us design better online learning environments. As such, we need to understand how these behavioral changes affect the intellectual content of the discussion. Does more equitable conversation necessarily mean better discussion? Do negative aspects of disinhibition (e.g., flaming) hurt educational discussions in chatrooms? How does the quality of a discussion in the classroom compare with the quality of a discussion in an online chatroom?

In this chapter, I present a quasi-experimental study in a professional ethics class that compares the quality of discussions in the face-to-face classroom with those online. Before describing this study, however, it is useful to consider the many ways we can go about analyzing "quality." In the next section, I describe a number of definitions and choose one to guide the analysis that follows.

4.1.1 Defining "Quality"

In the literature on small-group learning, "quality" is a word that means different things to different people. Cohen (1994), for example, describes four common definitions: (1) traditional academic achievement, (2) engagement in higher-order thinking skills, (3) equal status interaction, and (4) positive intergroup relations. As this list of definitions illustrates, it is important to distinguish between the quality of the *process* and the quality of the *content* when talking about the "quality" of an open-ended discussion.

At the *discussion process level*, we ask questions about the style and flow of interaction in the group. For example, do all students in the group participate equally (E. G. Cohen & Lotan, 1995)? How long do students sustain on-topic discussion (Guzdial & Turns, 2000)? What types of reasoning do students use when engaged in group discussions (Resnick, Salmon, Zeitz, Wathen, & Holowchak, 1993)? Does the discussion follow a classic initiate-respond-evaluate cycle (Chapter 3)? When focused on *discussion content*, we instead ask questions about the material covered in the discussion and resulting learning outcomes. Note that "content" does not necessarily equate to factual knowledge. The course aims may include behaviors and procedures to be learned, such as solving particular types of math problems (e.g., Barron, 2003) or integrating varying grammatical structures into speech (e.g., Kern, 1995). Asking questions about how well students carry out these target behaviors (i.e., discussion content) is often different from asking questions about how well students engage in discussion processes. Foreign language learning is one notable exception where discussion processes are also typical target behaviors. In learning domains where answers are not simply right or wrong, it is often tempting to focus on process questions before asking content questions. As Guzdial and Carroll (2002) point out, however, students frequently learn through discussions where the process seems to be less than ideal.

In addition to distinguishing between the process and the content of the discussion, it is also important to distinguish between quality on an individual level or on a group level. At an *individual level*, we can ask questions about individual behavior or learning from the group setting. For example, under which conditions does small group learning influence individual achievement test scores (Lou, Abrami, & d'Apollonia, 2001)? How do factors such as social status influence individual participation in group discussions (Chizhik, 2001)? Research into distributed cognition (Salomon, 1993) and activity theory (Engeström, Miettinen, & Punamäki, 1999), however, suggest that group interaction is an important component of individual performance, and that measures of individual learning/performance may not be able to fully capture the benefits of collaborative learning. As such, research into the quality of small group learning can also ask questions at the *group level*. For example, do groups create and encourage adequate opportunities for reflection (A. Cohen & Scardamalia, 1998)? Do groups help create social identities that encourage better learning (Job-Sluder & Barab, 2004)? Although individual learning is the ultimate goal of educational activities, it can be difficult to assess individual performance independent of the group on social tasks (Nasir, 2005).

In Chapter 3, I focused on asking questions about the *process* of the discussion. In the foreign language learning setting, instructors were concerned about encouraging language use. As long as the students were speaking in French, these instructors were not concerned with what they were talking about. In this domain, the process of the discussion was the learning goal. In many other domains, however, the content of the discussion is equally important. In this chapter, I focus on a content question at the group level in discussions in a professional ethics class. Specifically, do student groups consider ethical issues from multiple perspectives, and do they use evidence to support these perspectives? In starting with these questions, I do not deny the importance of asking individual or process questions. Rather, I start with this level of analysis because educational theory suggests that exploring multiple perspectives and using supporting evidence are important learning behaviors in group discussions. (See Chapter 2 for a more complete discussion of this literature.) In the next section, I describe the research setting—CS 4001: Computerization and Society—and show how the course aims, as expressed by the instructors, coincide nicely with these learning behaviors. After that, I present a quasi-experimental study that examines the "quality" of discussions in an online chat environment and in the classroom.

4.2 THE RESEARCH SETTING: CS 4001

In order to understand issues of conversational quality in online discussion environments, I began working with a professional ethics class at Georgia Tech known as *CS 4001: Computerization and Society*. CS 4001 was designed to expose upper-level, undergraduate computer science students to the types of ethical issues that they may have to professionally wrestle with one day.

When asked about their general goals for the course, instructors tended to emphasize the importance of helping students see the larger context surrounding the design and use of technology. As one instructor said:

> I wanted the kids to think more about the big picture of how technology affects the world as opposed to just thinking about the technology.

> So, what are the societal issues that surround the various technologies that we have developed or are developing or might be developed?

Other instructors echoed the same sentiment:

> [The goal was] to simply bring to the students' attention this natural ethical dilemma that you have as the professional in a profession of what you do and its impact on society.

Since computer science students can easily become focused exclusively on the machine itself, instructors felt that it was important for students to think about the social contexts of computers and their use.

More generally, however, instructors often emphasized the importance of encountering and engaging with multiple viewpoints about various ethical issues as a way of developing appropriate critical thinking skills:

> [I want students to] see different viewpoints on the same topic and get a little deeper understanding of why someone might think about something from a different perspective by being in the discussions in the small groups.

In reflecting on his experience, one course teaching assistant echoed these same ideas:

> I think that part of the class was about supporting their opinions or giving them the courage to have opinions and communicate those, but also trying to teach them how to acknowledge other

people's opinions and think critically about other people's opinions.

Other instructors also stressed the importance of multiple perspectives, but placed more emphasis on how those perspectives arise in conversation:

> I wanted students to actually interact with each other and actually come up with some good argumentation skills. ... I want them to sort of understand where people were coming from, and if they agreed, that's great. If they didn't, to be able to formulate their own reasons why they didn't agree. Not just because, "I don't agree." Why don't you agree? ... A halfway decent conversation might be two people fighting back and forth, as long as it's intelligent. If it's an intelligent debate, whether either side changed [doesn't matter].

> For me, a quality discussion would be one where, firstly, different points of view got expressed, different pieces of evidence. One of the things that I emphasized in the class was the idea of stakeholders and different kinds of stakeholders. So, certainly in some of these discussions, I encouraged the kids to take on the points of view of different stakeholders. So, a good discussion would be one where different people were taking on the perspectives of different stakeholders and then presumably having different points of view about something at least in some cases. ... So, a good discussion is one where different viewpoints come out, where rationales or arguments or reasons come out, where positive relationships or opposing relationships ..., getting beneath the surface of acts to understand the relationships

between facts and cause and effect, why different
points of view are held.

Instructors found it important for students to explore multiple sides of an ethical issue, but that exploration needed
to be structured so that it would be productive.
As one of the few humanistic courses required of Georgia
Tech's computer science majors, instructors took the emphasis on these argumentation skills further by making general
communication skills an explicit goal of the course:

> [I] emphasize communication skills in my class.
> Just as we want to focus on ethics, one of the
> shortcomings of computer scientists—at least to
> people to hire our students—is that they're awe-
> some programmers, but their interpersonal com-
> munication skills and their writing skills leave
> something to be desired. Where you have all of
> the education goals that you find on the syllabus,
> what you found on my syllabus was this addi-
> tional emphasis on developing communication
> skills and critical thinking.

In general, this course placed a much stronger emphasis
on written communication skills than did other classes.
In addition to a book on computer ethics, this course also
used a textbook that focused explicitly on argumentation.
Assignments included multiple, lengthy written essays.

4.2.1 The Role of Small Group Discussions
In Fall 1999, the College of Computing offered two sections
of CS 4001,[17] one with 30 students enrolled and the other

with 33 students. Although this was definitely large for a discussion class, it was still manageable for the instructor. By Spring 2004, there were 159 students enrolled in four sections of the course[18] for an average of forty students per section—a 152% increase in enrollment and a 33% increase in class size over five years! One instructor commented on how growing class size has affected his teaching:

> This course, when I started teaching it, had twenty or twenty-five students. Therefore, the ability of the professor to interact and generate discussion in kind of an oversized group was achievable. The course—because it was a required course and because we got a whole lot of students who needed to go through it—suddenly grew to forty or fifty, at which point, now you're into the lecture.

As a required course in an increasingly popular major, more and more students need to take the course, which makes it difficult to keep the class sizes reasonable. This instructor continued:

> This [course] is not about what I think, and I lecture to them, and they parrot it back to me. The course is about them thinking, expressing their thoughts, and having people agree/dis-agree, have different points of view, interact. As an instructor, the only way you can achieve that is getting them into smaller groups, planting that one or two question situation, and having them discuss it. … [Small groups have] a good work-able number so that everyone is engaged. Every-one has to express what they think. They can't hide in the back of the room. They can't *not* raise

> their hand. They can't trust that the professor
> won't remember their name, adding to their ano-
> nymity. They've got to discuss and interact with
> other computer science students.

Other instructors seconded the importance of small group
discussions as a way of encouraging discussion with a pro-
hibitively large class size:

> Things that worked well were breaking into little
> groups in class, having them talk about a particular
> set of issues, maybe giving them some questions
> to think about, and then having them report out.

In my observations of CS 4001 over multiple semesters,
I have found that all instructors use some form of small
group discussion.

Although instructors frequently relied on small group
discussions to deal with the challenging class size, my qualitative observations of these discussions indicated that the
quality varied significantly. In some cases, groups would
seem to stay on topic and have wonderful conversations,
especially if the instructor came by to provoke discussion. In other cases, however, students had not completed
assigned background readings or simply were not engaged
by the discussion topic. My informal assessment was that
quality varied somewhat dramatically from group to group
and discussion to discussion. In general, the instructors
seconded this observation:

> I noted that some students, some groups would
> say, "Ok. I've answered all of the questions or

said everything there is to say." And they would
start talking about something else before I would
call everyone back together, rather than staying
on topic, staying on subject.

Some questions would [generate discussion] and
some wouldn't. By the same token, sometimes
the same question would work for one semester
and it might not work the next. ... [The quality
of group discussions was] all over the map.

With the instructor splitting his or her attention between
eight or nine discussion groups, it was impossible to ensure
that all groups have the best possible conversation. Before
describing these small group discussions any further, it is
useful to take some time to look at a typical class section
using small group discussion.

4.2.2 A Typical Class Session

This section presents a description of a typical class session using small group discussion in CS 4001. This
description is a composition of events drawn from observations over the course of a semester. Although I spent
three semesters observing up to three sections of this class
per semester, I choose to focus on this one particular class
section because it involves the same instructor—Ed, an
experienced instructor who had taught this course many
times since its creation—as the more experimental study
described below. Ed, however, is fairly representative of
the four instructors observed. I offer this narrative to provide a sense of this class before delving into the details of
problems and methods.

4.2.2.1 Arrival

The physical design of the classroom is somewhat long and narrow. Although desks are never perfectly arranged in neat rows, there are approximately eight rows of five desks each going from the front of the room to the back. At the front of the room is a slightly raised stage that effectively separates the instructor's area from that of the students. On this stage is a makeshift desk, consisting of a table and one chair, and a podium that contains audio/visual equipment. The room appears to have been created when two rooms were joined during the building's last renovations, probably during the 1970s. As such, it has two doors: one at the front of the room and one about two-thirds of the way toward the back. There is a row without desks at the second door so that students may easily cross from one side of the room to the other. This effectively divides the desks into two sections. The front portion of the room contains five rows of five desks, and the rear portion contains three rows of five desks.

Although a couple of students arrive around noon, most students show up between noon and 12:10 PM. Officially this class starts at 12:05 PM, but, in practice, the class seldom starts on time. Students who enter the front door tend to sit near the front of the room. Students who enter the rear door tend to sit in the back of the room. Rarely do students enter the front and cross to the rear or enter the rear and walk to the front. As such, the room tends to fill in from these two doors, leaving the third row largely empty. On this particular day, twenty-seven students were there by the time class started. Five others arrived shortly after the start of class.

Typical of the gender distribution in computer science at Georgia Tech, only five of these thirty-two students are female. The women's behavior in this course, however, is almost identical to the men. The women's desks appear to be randomly distributed; no two women sit near each other. Some sit in the front of the room; some sit in the back. Some women actively participate in discussions; some try to avoid being called on. In short, gender appears to be a non-issue. As one woman in the class put it, "I just personally never had a problem, but I think it's because I don't let being a woman affect the way I act." Although gender issues can certainly be problematic in computer science (Margolis & Fisher, 2002), these particular women who have survived into their senior year in college do not perceive gender issues as affecting this class.

Ethnic issues, however, appear more troublesome in this course. Although there were exceptions, in general, Caucasian students sat close to the front and middle of the room. Meanwhile, minority and foreign students tended to cluster toward the back of the room or toward the edges. Not surprisingly, the students toward the front and middle of the room tended to speak more often than students toward the back or the edges of the room.[19]

On this particular day, the course instructor, Ed, arrives a little early, at noon, and begins writing an overview of the next couple of weeks on the board. Tony, the teaching assistant for the course, is sitting next to me in the back of the room observing everything that is going on. While we are sitting there, one of the students approaches him. Jason, a typically well-meaning, conscientious student, "did not wish to start any rumors," but he wanted to let Tony know that Georgia Tech might declare a "snow day" the coming Friday. According to Jason, Georgia Tech declared a snow day in 1990 when the basketball team made it into the Final Four of the NCAA tournament. Since Georgia Tech's basketball team had made it into the Final Four again, Jason wanted Tony to be aware that class may be officially canceled on Friday. Tony seemed amused, but thanked the student, and Jason returned to his seat.

4.2.2.2 Introductory Lecture
Despite arriving early, Ed still does not begin the class until 12:09 PM. He spends the next eleven minutes discussing the upcoming group project and how it fits into the class schedule for the next couple of weeks. In this project, he wants students to work in groups of four. Ed does not assign the groups, but the students must ensure that they do not work with someone whom they collaborated with on the previous group project. On this project, students must choose one of three provided cases to do a case study analysis. Although Therac-25, which was covered earlier in class, is one of the potential cases that students can use, Ed points out that students choosing this topic must move significantly beyond the previous analysis in their papers. One particularly important way for students to do that is covering ways that the system failed technically, in addition to the social failures that were discussed in class.

During this discussion of the group project, Jason raised his hand and informed Ed about the potential snow day on Friday. Again, Jason stressed that he "did not want to start any rumors." Ed basically discounted this, but seemed amused nonetheless. He commented, "That'd be kind of cool, wouldn't it? A snow day in April."

4.2.2.3 Small Group Discussion

After covering the introductory material, Ed had the students divide into groups of approximately four people at 12:20 PM. He wanted these groups to consider the implications of using simulations instead of crash tests to determine the safety of cars. Lara, Cody, Todd, and Seth were seated close together, so they formed a group and began considering this topic. Although Lara, Cody, and Todd face one another and lean in, Seth angles his body away from this group. Not surprisingly, Seth also participates less frequently than the other students in the group. More importantly, it seemed that none of the others addressed Seth when they spoke. Rather, Lara, Cody, and Todd seemed to primarily make eye contact with one another. Even when Seth did speak to the group, however, the others rarely looked at him. When the others spoke, however, everyone looked at the speaker. Often, the others would make direct eye contact with Seth when they responded to his statements.

After twenty minutes, the group felt that they had largely exhausted the discussion questions that Ed had set forth. Since they felt that they were done with the discussion, they spent a while talking about various tangential topics like the movie *The Matrix* and wearing green for St. Patrick's Day. After several more minutes, Seth commented that they should try to figure out if they have a consensus since the groups needed to post their conclusions on the class's online discussion space. Because he said something, the group decided that Seth should be the scribe, a role that he tries to avoid because of poor handwriting. While coming up with the consensus, Lara's use of eye gaze was particularly interesting. When answering definitively, she looked directly at Seth, the scribe. When questioning the group decision, however, she looked at Cody and Todd, but not Seth.

4.2.2.4 Wrap-Up/Report Out

At 12:48 PM, Ed stopped the group discussion and had the students briefly report on their ideas. At the very end of class, Tony, the TA, gave the students some important guidelines for their upcoming papers. These guidelines were basic writing skills like citing sources and how to make a logical argument. While Tony was talking, however, there was a lot of movement as students packed up their belongings and prepared to leave the room. At 12:57 PM, the class ended and students rushed out.

4.2.3 The Everyday Problems
of Participation in CS 4001

As this typical day illustrates, even the best instructors struggle with certain aspects of the course. With ambitious learning objectives, overflowing class size, and widely varying student motivation, this class can be especially daunting, even for experienced instructors. In this section, I review each of these challenges in a little more detail.

The following section looks at a pilot study into how technology might help.

4.2.3.1 Too Little Time

As a discussion-oriented class, instructors often find time constraints to be a significant challenge. By the time the instructor begins class and covers the introductory material, he or she often finds that little time remains for discussion. As one student put it:

> The time that's required for set up, introducing the discussion, and then conclusion makes it so that you can get far less in than you think with a 50 minute period. ... You have very little time in there for discussion.

On multiple occasions, I observed instructors run longer than expected during their discussions of the introductory material. By the time they wrapped up the introduction, the class period was halfway over. When this happened, instructors frequently decided to not engage in small group discussions, but rather to cover the material as a whole-class discussion.

The instructors also face a second challenge related to time: there is simply too much material to cover during the semester. There are two primary course objectives: (1) learning about social issues relating to computing and (2) learning about argumentation as a literary form. This course is designed so that argumentation is learned in the context of social issues in computing, but instructors still face the difficult choice of determining which topics to focus on and which ones to ignore.[20] Ed's course, for example, gives greater emphasis to helping students understand the social issues surrounding computing, whereas other instructors spend more time on teaching argumentation skills. With this much potential material to cover, it is not uncommon for students to spend only one day on large topics such as privacy.

4.2.3.2 Class Size

As I discussed above, the class size for CS 4001 is simply too large for everyone to be able to participate in a general class discussion. When the department introduced this course, there were only a limited number of students majoring in computer science. Over the years, however, the number of majors has grown at a faster rate than the teaching faculty. As such, class enrollment typically hovers around 40 students in each of the three or four sections of the course offered each semester. If a typical class session lasts for 50 minutes and there are 40 students, it is mathematically impossible for everyone to participate in a meaningful way unless the instructors use small group discussions.

4.2.3.3 Motivation

> I think [that what students got out of the class] varied a whole lot based on where the students were coming from. I think with a few of the students, they didn't need the course because they already were very much attuned to the issues,

to the considerations, to what's going on in the world around them. For some students, they didn't give a darn. ... And, then, there's all the way in between. I think, in some cases, people really woke up to more thinking about broader issues and will just do that on their own. (One instructor's reflection on learning in his class).

In addition to having too many students and too much material to cover, instructors for CS 4001 must also struggle with motivational interests. As a required course with no technical content, a handful of students in any class simply do not see the point. These students view the class as one more hoop that they have to jump through to get their degree. As such, they attempt to get by with as little mental engagement and effort as possible. At the other end of the spectrum, however, there are always a handful of students who are incredibly enthusiastic about the course material. These students have opinions on everything, and usually want to contribute to any group discussion. These students frequently talk over quieter students or those without such strong opinions. Finally, the majority of students lie in the middle; they are not excited about being in the class, but they're willing to participate as long as the material is reasonably engaging. Instructors frequently struggle with how to lead the class so that all three populations of students learn something meaningful.

4.2.4 Behavioral Changes in Online Pilot Studies
Early pilot work with the CS 4001 class aimed at establishing (a) that the findings from the foreign language learning

domain would carry over to this new learning domain and
(b) that there was reason to believe that these discussions
would be educationally beneficial. In the online discussions, I observed that all students seemed to participate
a significant amount in the online environment. I should
point out, however, that groups in this new environment
consisted of only three or four students instead of the typical six or seven in my research with IRC Français. Informal
observations of discussions in face-to-face settings suggest
that groups this small often have more equitable participation, regardless of medium.

However, student interviews also suggested that some
felt reduced inhibitions in the online environment. In one
student's words:

> For me, it's easier to talk online than it is in per-
> son because, when you're in person, you kind
> of have to form your thoughts in real time. You
> think and then you have to say it. If you mess up,
> you can't hit backspace anymore. Whereas in an
> online forum, I can sit and formulate a thought.
> No one expects me to answer immediately. When
> they ask me a question, I can sit and think for 30
> seconds. I think the online discussions are actu-
> ally a little more productive because of that.

As this student expresses, having a small delay during
which to collect his thoughts allowed him to feel more
comfortable expressing himself in the online environment.
Other students echoed this same idea:

I thought through what I was going to say a lot more in the online discussions before I said it. ... So, I had my thoughts a little more organized.

From these observations and interviews, there was reason to believe that the same social psychological phenomena that I observed in Chapter 3 were acting in this new learning domain. Also, there was a suggestion that students might have an educationally beneficial experience online.

4.3 QUASI-EXPERIMENTAL METHOD

4.3.1 Data Collected
To explore how online and face-to-face groups differ in the quality of their discussion content, I worked with Ed, an instructor who was teaching two course sections during the same semester. For this study, Ed agreed to conduct four class sessions in a row using small-group discussions, which alternated between the face-to-face classroom and a fairly standard online chat environment. As Table 2 shows, the students in the first class met in a chatroom on Day 2 and Day 3. The other days were in the face-to-face classroom. Likewise, the students in the second class met online on Day 1 and Day 4, and face-to-face on Day 2 and Day 3.[21] Students were randomly assigned to groups, which remained constant throughout the study.

Table 2. Medium Used in Each Class Session

	Day 1	Day 2	Day 3	Day 4
Class A	Face-to-Face	Online	Online	Face-to-Face
Class B	Online	Face-to-Face	Face-to-Face	Online

In the face-to-face environment, Ed conducted the class as he normally did. After some introductory comments, he divided the students into groups, which were to discuss a specified ethical scenario relating to the day's broader ethical topic. For example, in dealing with the general topic of privacy, one discussion focused on the legal and ethical issues surrounding the use of new police surveillance technologies, such as facial recognition and thermal imaging. To support these discussions, Ed gave the students a handout with typically five or six questions to address. Students discussed the assigned topics until Ed sensed that the discussion was drawing to an end. At that point, he led the students in a whole-class discussion about their group conversations until the end of the period. I videotaped and transcribed the small group interactions of seven groups (4 in Class A and 3 in Class B) for this study.

In the online environment, Ed had no interaction with the students during the assigned class period, which presents a methodological confound that I discuss in more detail below. Instead, students logged onto a web-based, text-chat client during regular class time. The software automatically divided students into their assigned groups. Otherwise, it was a standard web-based IRC chat client.

Once online, students discussed the same topics as the face-to-face groups. When they completed their discussions, students logged off and were done for the day. At the beginning of the following classroom session, Ed conducted a whole-group discussion on the scenario for the online students. The chat software automatically saved transcripts of the discussions from the target groups for later analysis.

During these four class periods, discussions focused mainly on topics related to privacy. On the first day, students considered a scenario in which a mother has stumbled across her college-aged daughter's blog. Questions focused on whether or not the daughter had a right to expect some level of privacy from her mother. A related question asked students to consider how the scenario might change if it were an employee/employer relationship. The second day's discussion presented students with a scenario in which a company's employees were accessing private customer information from the company's database. Students explored the implications for various stakeholders, appropriate courses of action, and the responsibilities of the database designer for protecting against such unauthorized access. The third discussion focused on companies monitoring employees' actions for productivity or safety. As an extension, students were asked to consider the implications of companies monitoring customers, not employees. In the final assignment, students discussed the implications of new police surveillance techniques, such as thermal imaging and video-based facial recognition. Ed developed all of these assignments. The exact discussion instructions are listed in Appendix A.

Because of some technical problems that caused the loss of 3.5 online transcripts,[22] I obtained transcripts from 14 face-to-face classroom discussions and 10.5 online classroom discussions. In the next section, I describe a coding scheme developed to analyze the quality of discussions in each of these media.

4.3.2 Quantifying "Quality"

The question becomes, how do we quantitatively evaluate the content of a small group discussion? There are three traditional methodological approaches to studying argumentation, which offer some guidance. First, many researchers rely on case studies and other microanalyses to examine the detailed ways that argumentation varies from setting to setting (e.g., Rafal, 1996; Schwarz & Glassner, 2003). Although there are certainly strengths to this approach, it does not allow us to easily quantify differences between environments.

The second methodological approach relies on coding conversational transcripts for types of dialog moves. Researchers using this approach have developed a number of unique coding schemes (Resnick, Salmon, Zeitz, Wathen, & Holowchak, 1993; Andriessen, Erkens, van de Laak, Peters, & Coirier, 2003; Jermann & Dillenbourg, 2003; van Bruggen & Kirschner, 2003; Veerman, 2003), most featuring codes that focus on the development and evoluation of ideas, such as *hypothesis presentation, elaboration,* and *questioning.*This methodological approach works well to evaluate knowledge building through argumentative discourse (Resnick, Salmon, Zeitz, Wathen, &

Holowchak, 1993). Andriessen (2006), however, points out that these types of coding schemes typically fail to capture the back-and-forth of ideas that occurs in group discussions. In fact, frequently, research using these coding schemes relies on dyadic discussion where pairs are given a position to argue (Andriessen, Erkens, van de Laak, Peters, & Coirier, 2003) or are constructed to encourage disagreement (e.g., de Vries, Lund, & Baker, 2002; Jermann & Dillenbourg, 2003). As such, there's reason to believe that this method (a) would not capture well the content of discussions and (b) would be difficult to adapt to three or four person groups engaged in problem solving.[23]

The final common methodological approach—comparisons against an "ideal" answer—holds promise, but still presents a number of difficulties. In this approach, researchers develop an answer against which they measure all other discussions. In many cases, this "ideal" answer is the scientifically correct one. For example, Barron (2003) looked at whether or not small groups correctly solved mathematics problems and Baker (2003) examined the development of correct scientific mental models of sound during small group discussion. This approach has also been used to study group discussion around more open-ended, ill-defined problems in social science, such as the ones discussed in the CS 4001 class. Suthers and Hundhausen (2003), for example, used experts to develop an "ideal" answer to their open-ended problem. As they discovered, however, students invariably advocated positions and used evidence that was not included in their "ideal" answer. When this occurred, they were forced to deal with the students' answers in ad hoc ways.

In many ways, comparing student discussions against an "ideal" criterion offers an excellent way to quantify the quality of small group discussions. The challenge, however, lies in developing an appropriate "ideal" answer that includes all of the possible legitimate perspectives that students might express. Since this is a nearly intractable problem, I suggest that a different approach might be suitable. Instead of creating an "ideal" answer to use as a standard of comparison, I suggest that we can create an "aggregate" answer that can work in much the same way. In the next section, I present a new method that uses grounded theory (Glaser & Strauss, 1967; Strauss & Corbin, 1998) to develop an aggregate answer based on the content of student discussions. Then, I compare individual group discussions against this aggregate answer to describe the quality of each discussion. Although this method does not draw distinctions between "better" and "worse" perspectives, I will show that it seems to capture our qualitative notions of better and worse discussions without problematic ad hoc approaches to the data.

4.3.3 Developing a Standard of Comparison
Both the goals for this course and educational theory emphasize the importance of (a) being able to see ethical dilemmas from a variety of different perspectives and (b) being able to use evidence to support each of these perspectives in arriving at an appropriate course of action. In order to quantify this, I first developed an aggregate standard of comparison based on the perspectives and evidence used by all groups. By aggregating all of the student perspectives

and evidence into one "idealized" answer, I generated a standard of comparison that captured the diversity of the group discussions, yet fully encompassed all perspectives expressed in the class. For each group, I used content analysis to read through the discussion transcript and identified all of the perspectives presented and the evidence or logic used to support these perspectives. At this point, I did not take into account the accuracy or relative strength of any given argument[24]; instead, I merely recorded any argument that a group made. I listed each argument or piece of evidence on a note card that also identified the group and question.

Once I had identified all of the arguments from each group on a given topic, I used techniques from grounded theory (Turner, 1981; Strauss & Corbin, 1998) to cluster diverse arguments into similar perspectives and similar evidence. In the first question of the first day of discussion, for example, each group made an argument that I classified as "bloggers have no right to expect privacy" because "there are technical means that could have been used to ensure privacy":

(Group 1, Day 1, Face-to-face)[25]
Andy: I think the only way to sort of keep people out is if I put some sort of a disclaimer or maybe username and password login. Some kind of thing in there where it said... where you know that you're only allowed to view this if they've given you permission in some way. A disclaimer or a password or a user logon, something like that. But, if it's just click through...

(Group 2, Day 1, Face-to-face)

William: They're posting it publicly. They're not... It's not like it's a password protected site or anything.

[...]

Aaron: If you had a journal, I bet you could password protect it. One of those friends only things or something like that. You'll have an expectation of privacy, but, I mean, <unintelligible>. You have an expectation of privacy from certain people in that only you have an all or nothing thing.

Niraj: I mean, that's true that whoever she told, she couldn't expect privacy from them, but there could be thirty people out there who haven't asked, like in this case.

(Group 3, Day 1, Face-to-face)

John: If you don't put something password protect or whatever on the Internet, it's wide open. And, even sometimes when it's password protected, it's still accessible.

(Group 4, Day 1, Face-to-face)

Edward: So, they should not consider what they have on their blogs to be private, anyway, unless perhaps they had some sort of a password. You could do that. You can, say, give all your friends a login.

(Group 5, Day 1, Online)

```
Ben: yeah, plus most blogs have the option of
only allowing registered friends to view it
Ben: so they should use that instead
```

(Group 6, Day 1, Online)

Eric: they only way you could possibly expect it to be private is if you had some sort of authentication system

(Group 7, Day 1, Online)

Chris: if you don't put limits on who can read it, then its fair game

Although all of the groups made the argument that there are technical means of obtaining privacy, which bloggers should use in order to have a reasonable expectation of privacy, they rarely put it in those terms. In fact, there are some nuanced differences between each group's take on this issue, which were lost because of this analysis technique. In this example, all of these discussions were coded as taking the perspective that bloggers should have no expectation of privacy. They were further coded as using the evidence that there are technical means of ensuring privacy.

The clusters of perspectives and evidence became the aggregated, idealized answer. Because this method identified all of the student answers first, this aggregated list incorporated all of the perspectives and evidence used. In other words, the student groups did not identify any perspective or evidence that was not included on the aggregated answer list. Through identifying which perspectives each group took, the aggregated list allowed me to make comparisons between the groups.

4.3.4 "Grading" the Discussions

Having developed this aggregated argument to use as the standard of comparison, I had to evaluate how closely individual discussions matched with this standard. For each group discussion, I first identified which perspectives and evidence from the aggregate list were used in that discussion. This is in keeping with how other researchers have used the "ideal" answer method in argumentation research (e.g., M. W. Keefer, Zeitz, & Resnick, 2000; Baker, 2003; Suthers & Hundhausen, 2003). Because of the unique contexts of individual research projects, however, researchers tend to use different methods at this point to generate a quantitative "grade(s)" for the discussion. For this study, I generated an algorithm that balanced the use of perspectives with the use of evidence. As I will show below, the results of this method are consistent with more simplistic measures such as counting the number of perspectives or the amount of evidence used. This algorithm, however, more fully captures the balance between perspectives and evidence supporting these perspectives.

To quantify this information, I first asked the instructor to assign weights to each question, as if each discussion topic had been a test. For example, in the first discussion on privacy in blogs, Ed said that the first and second questions should each be worth twenty points while the third question should be worth only five points.

To assign credit for each question, I gave each potential perspective equal weight. For example, if a question was worth 20 points and four perspectives were expressed on the aggregated list, each individual perspective was worth five points. Students received half of the credit assigned to a perspective if they simply stated that viewpoint and provided no other supporting evidence. The remaining half of the credit was equally divided between all of the available evidence. This scoring metric is not without flaws; some perspectives and some pieces of supporting evidence are more valid than others from an expert's perspective, but all are treated equally in this metric. In most cases, however, it is quite difficult to quantify the relative merits of one perspective against another or one piece of evidence against another. Because it is impossible to assess exactly how much stronger one perspective is over another, I chose to allow everything to have an equal weight.

As an example of this scoring metric, consider Group Three's answers to Question 2 on the second scenario on Day 2. This question was worth 10 points, and asked students to consider the responsibilities of a software development/design consultant in foreseeing the potential security risks during the development of a system for accessing customers' credit information. See Appendix A for the exact questions and the aggregated student answers.

For this question, the class had identified four perspectives on the aggregate list: (1) consultants do have a responsibility to look for potential security risks, (2) consultants do not have such a responsibility, (3) responsibility is shared between the consultant and the company, and (4) regardless of whether or not there is an ethical responsibility, it is just good business practice for the consultant to look for potential security risks. Because there were four perspectives identified and 10 points allocated to this question, each perspective was worth 2.5 points. On the first perspective (i.e., consultants have a responsibility for security issues), Group Three used two of the three pieces of supporting evidence. Specifically, they argue that one person cannot reasonably foresee all potential problems and they argue that consultants are only obligated to follow the design guidelines given to them.

Therefore, they received 1.25 points credit for stating this perspective and another 0.83 points credit (two-thirds of the remaining 1.25 points) for their use of evidence, giving them 2.08 points credit (out of 2.5 possible) for this perspective. Similarly, they identified the third perspective and two of four pieces of evidence for it, giving them another 1.88 points credit. Group Three did not identify either of the remaining perspectives voiced by other groups. This earned Group Three a total of 3.96 points credit (out of 10 points) for this question, which gave them the lowest grade in the class on this question.

Having assigned a score in this way, I could not compare scores from one day to the next. There was no way of ensuring that a score of 75 on one topic was equivalent to a score of 75 on another topic. To solve this problem, I normalized each day's "grades" by computing a z-score. Essentially, a z-score identifies the distance—in terms of standard deviations—from the mean. In other words, if a group received a z-score of 1.0, they were one standard deviation above the average score for that discussion. Likewise, negative z-scores represent the distance below the mean for any given discussion. By converting to z-scores, I was able to make comparisons from one discussion to the next.

4.3.5 Relative Versus Absolute Scores

Note that z-scores provide relative, not absolute, weights. In other words, a high z-score says that one group's discussion was better along the measured dimensions than the other groups' discussions on that topic. A high z-score does not say, however, whether or not the discussion was actually "good" in the instructor's or another expert's opinion. Nonetheless, there is reason to believe that the z-scores roughly correspond with our qualitative notions of "good" versus "poor" discussions. To illustrate this, consider how Group 3 ($z_{\text{Group 3}}$ = −1.05) and Group 6 ($z_{\text{Group 6}}$ = 1.44) handled Question 6 (Should employers fire employees over comments made on a personal blog?) on the first day of discussion. The exact assignment can be found in Appendix A; complete transcripts of both of these conversations can be found in Appendix B.

In presenting these two contrasting discussions, I do not suggest that Group 6's discussion is perfect nor do I suggest that Group 3's discussion is without merit. Instead, I try to show that, in general, Group 6's discussion is quite good. Likewise, Group 3's discussion has significant room for improvement. I offer these two examples to illustrate that the grading metric used in this chapter reasonably captures our notions of the qualitative merit of an educational discussion. Despite imperfections in the grading metric, it appears to capture some part of our notions of "quality."

Question 6, worth 30 points, asked the students to consider a related situation in which an employer wants to fire an employee over the content of a personal blog. In the relatively "good" discussion, Group 6 spent a significant amount of time talking about this issue. In their discussion, they tended to focus on two related questions: Is it right for an employer to read an employee's blog? And, should an employer fire an employee over the content of the blog? In discussing these two questions, Group 6 largely agreed that the current legal system allows both, so they focused more on the ethicality of each action.

Regarding whether or not employers should read employee blogs, this group felt that there was a distinction between accidentally stumbling across a blog and actively searching for a blog. Group 6 felt that accidentally stumbling across a blog was similar to an employer overhearing conversation—whether in the next cubicle or walking by someone on a street corner. Searching for employee blogs, however, represented an unreasonable intrusion of work into the personal lives of employees.

Regarding whether or not employers should fire employees over the content of their blogs, Group 6 felt that this was only acceptable when the content of the blog reflected negatively on the company. Although this certainly applied for corporate sponsored blogs and negative comments made about the company on a personal blog, Group 6 put a more nuanced spin on the issue. In particular, they focused on times when employees act, or are perceived to act, as a company representative. They pointed out that corporate management and military personnel in uniform are both perceived to act as representatives of their organizations, even if they are voicing strictly personal opinions. Therefore, they felt that employees who are perceived to be representatives for the company, whether or not this perception is warranted, should be held to different standards than other employees. Although Group 3 touched on some of these same issues, they had a much less nuanced discussion, which lasted for only 12 turns. Essentially, this group argued that the public nature of blogs means that employers are free to read their content, even if it is not directly related to the workplace. Then, the group felt that the employer has a right to fire employees based on this content, although they did note the employer's actions should be in keeping with the company's policies.

As these two discussions illustrate, Group 6 had a much more thorough discussion of the relationship between personal blogs and the workplace than did Group 3. Both groups reached similar general conclusions that employers can fire employees over the content of personal blogs, but Group 6 also explored issues such as when an employer should ethically examine a personal blog and how a blurred relationship can arise between work and personal lives. Although both discussions have room for improvement, Group 6's discussion is much closer to what we would hope to see in these conversations.

4.4 RESULTS

Results from this analysis are presented in Figure 4, with more details available in Table 3. Briefly, these data suggest that discussions online might be a little bit worse than discussions in the classroom, but that other factors probably influence these discussions much more than media choice.

As Figure 4 shows, some groups (e.g., Group 5) seem to do much better in the face-to-face classroom than online. Other groups (e.g., Group 6), however, perform much better in the online environment than they do in the classroom. Still other groups (e.g., Group 2) seem to have more day-to-day variance than medium-based variance. This suggests that other factors are more likely to explain these patterns than medium effects. The evidence also suggests that groups that perform poorly at identifying various perspectives also tend to perform poorly when presenting evidence.

As Table 3 shows, students seem to take twice as long to convey their ideas in the online environment than they do in the classroom. Online discussions of an equivalent quality

Figure 4. Comparing the Quality of Discussion Content

	Group 1	Group 2	Group 3	Group 4	Group 5	Group 6	Group 7
Topic 1	0.27	0.84	-1.05	0.40	-0.80	1.44	-1.11
Topic 2	-1.06	-0.27	-0.46	0.00	1.88	-0.23	0.14
Topic 3	-0.08	1.50	-0.25	-1.61	0.81	-0.61	0.25
Topic 4	0.74	1.01	-1.39	-0.65	0.00	0.28	0.00

■ Online Conversation
▨ Face-to-Face Conversation

Table 3. Details for Each Discussion

	Group ID	Condition	Number of Participants	Duration of On-Topic Discussion	Z-Score	Number of Perspectives Expressed	Amount of Evidence Used
Day 1							
	1	f2f	4	16 min	0.27	15	21
	2	f2f	3	27 min	0.84	15	21
	3	f2f	4	15 min	-1.05	11	18
	4	f2f	3	24 min	0.40	14	25
	5	online	4	48 min	-0.80	13	19
	6	online	4*	50 min	1.44	15	23
	7	online	4	40 min	-1.11	11	21
Day 2							
	1	online	2	20 min	-1.06	18	10
	2	online	3	45 min**	-0.27	11	11
	3	online	4	76 min	-0.46	18	20
	5	f2f	3	21 min	1.88	30	32
	6	f2f	4	15 min	-0.23	20	23
	7	f2f	4	10 min	0.14	19	15

(continued)

Table 3. (continued) Details for Each Discussion

Group ID	Condition	Number of Participants	Duration of On-Topic Discussion	Z-Score	Number of Perspectives Expressed	Amount of Evidence Used
Day 3						
1	online	4	40 min	-0.08	14	23
2	online	4*	60 min	1.50	18	33
3	online	4	60 min	-0.25	13	23
4	online	3	40 min	-1.61	11	20
5	f2f	3	25 min	0.81	17	31
6	f2f	3	10 min	-0.61	15	27
7	f2f	2	24 min	0.25	26	32
Day 4						
1	f2f	4	31 min	0.74	14	23
2	f2f	3	34 min	1.01	15	29
3	f2f	4*	20 min	-1.39	8	14
4	f2f	3	18 min	-0.65	12	18
6	online	3	30 min	0.28	12	17

*These discussions began with three group members. The fourth group member joined toward the end of the conversation.

**This discussion was not able to finish because of technical problems.

to face-to-face conversations required twice as long. This occurred partly because there is generally a slower pace to this type of online interaction (i.e., typing is typically slower than speaking), but also because students divide their attention between the conversation and other aspects of their environment (e.g., reading email, looking up additional information online, making a sandwich for lunch). These two factors may promote a cycle where the slower pace promotes splitting attention, which causes a slower pace, etc. There are some pedagogical and design techniques that can alleviate this, but instructors should be aware that the pace of conversation differs significantly online. Below, I describe each of these findings in more detail.

4.4.1 Media Effects Matter Relatively Little

Based on these data, there is some evidence that suggests that the medium might have a minor impact on the quality of discussions in this class, but that other factors (i.e., group dynamics) play a more important role. Eight of the eleven online discussions were below average; only five of fourteen face-to-face discussions were below average. The average online z-score was -0.22 (st.dev = 0.99), while the average face-to-face z-score was 0.17 (st.dev = 0.89). Although there is suggestive evidence of a trend, this difference is not significant ($p = 0.31$ using a two-tailed T-test with equal variance).[26]

Note that a finding of no-significant-difference is an inconclusive finding. Informal qualitative analysis, however, suggests that the quality of the discussion content seemed comparable in both conditions. Although I found that participation increased online in the foreign language learning setting (i.e., the *process* was better online), we would predict that the *content* of online interaction would not achieve the same quality as face-to-face conversation given the general reputation of chat systems. It is, therefore, somewhat surprising that little difference appears to exist.

Although further research is needed to determine whether or not quality differences actually exist between these media, the patterns of variation suggest that other factors likely play more important roles. The standard deviation of these z-scores says much about the importance of the potential group differences within these experimental conditions. There is so much variability in these conditions that it is impossible to distinguish any real differences between the conditions from the noise in the results. This suggests that other factors probably have much more influence than the medium.

4.4.2 Use of Perspectives and Evidence

Not surprisingly, results indicate that the number of perspectives expressed (again, converted to z-scores) correlate strongly with the overall score ($r = 0.89$). (See Table 3 for details). The amount of evidence used also correlated strongly with both the overall score ($r = 0.79$) and the number of perspectives expressed ($r = 0.79$). In other words, the best groups explored more perspectives and used more evidence than poorer performing groups. When taking the number of perspectives expressed into account, however, the amount of evidence used seems to have no impact on overall score. There is no correlation between the amount of evidence used per perspective and the overall score (r = 0.06). Although there is no significant difference between the amount of evidence per perspective used online and in the face-to-face classroom (p = 0.21 using a two-tailed t-test with equal variance), there is a potential trend suggesting that students online might use less evidence per perspective (mean = –0.27; st.dev = 0.94) than students in the classroom (mean = 0.21; st.dev = 0.91). Further research is needed to determine the validity of this trend.

4.4.3 Time on Task

Although that there is no difference between the quality of the discussions in the online and face-to-face conditions, it does take students in the online condition significantly longer to express these ideas (p < 0.001 using a one-tailed T-test assuming unequal variance). As Table 4 shows, in the face-to-face condition, students discussed the topic for an average of 20.68 minutes (st.dev = 7.29). Online, discussions of the topic lasted for 46.27 minutes (st.dev = 15.34). In the online environment, it took the students twice as much time to express their ideas. Note that discussions in both media involved some off-topic conversation, which has been removed from this analysis.

Table 4. Length of Conversations

	Average On-Topic Conversation Length
Face-to-Face	20.68 minutes (st.dev = 7.29)
Online	46.27 minutes (st.dev = 15.34)

Why does it take students so much longer to discuss a topic online than face-to-face? One answer is that it is simply easier to convey a nuanced idea quickly through the richness of face-to-face communication. For example, in Weisband's (1992) research on decision-making, she found that face-to-face and computer-mediated discussion groups exchanged roughly the same number of messages over the course of a discussion, but that online groups exchanged messages more slowly and required more time. Similarly, Walther and Anderson (1994) found that online decision-making groups reveal similar amounts of interpersonal information as face-to-face groups, but that online groups again require more time.

This explanation, however, only seems to tell part of the story. In this study, students in the face-to-face classroom spoke an average of 155.77 words per minute (st.dev = 39.52), which is consistent with the literature on face-to-face discussions (e.g., Darragh & Witten, 1992). A separate research study conducted with this same population of students has found that these students type approximately 80 words per minute each in a transcription task (Clarkson, Clawson, Lyons, & Starner, 2005). It is not clear how applicable this typing rate is to a group discussion task, but it is reasonable to assume 3–4 students who can compose messages in parallel might generate a total of 80 words per minute. If word count was consistent in each environment, the online discussions should last 40 minutes, which they did.

We know from linguistic research, however, that "unnecessary" linguistic information is typically dropped from online discussions (Collot & Belmore, 1996; Condon & Cech, 1996; Werry, 1996; Yates, 1996). It is not surprising, then, to discover that online conversations used fewer words (mean = 1812.64; st.dev = 715.91) than face-to-face discussions (mean = 3213.14; st.dev = 1335.72). As such, we should expect online discussions to last only 22 minutes. It is surprising, however, to find out that the 3–4 participants—each of whom has a typing rate of approximately 80 words per minute—only generated 39.92 words per minutes (st.dev = 10.10) in the online environment. In other words, each student involved in a group discussion contributed only ten to thirteen words per minute. Although it does take longer to type a message than it does to say it, this explanation does not seem to completely account for the additional time needed in the chat environment. In fact, there is only a mild correlation between a group's score and the number of words used ($r_{face-to-face}$ = 0.47; r_{online} = 0.56).

Because of the naturalistic setting for this type of research, a second factor played an important role in the time required for online discussions: students conversing online did not give the conversation their complete attention. In some cases, they looked up additional, relevant information through the internet, as in the following discussion:

1. **Ben:** what if meeting the quota would cause a safety risk?
2. **Carlos:** or work for a competitor
3. **Carlos:** then notify osha
4. **Jonathan:** what's that stand for

5. **Mike:** oh i forget
6. **Jonathan:** Occupational Safety and Health Ad-
   ministration
7. **Jonathan:** thanks google define:
8. **Mike:** Occupational Safety and Health Admin-
   istration
9. **Mike:** gg wikipedia

In this example, the students are able to quickly grab a small amount of information off the web. During the pilot studies, one student commented on this behavior explicitly:

> I prefer to talk online or via email than in person because you get the time to think before you say something, and also because you have all this auxiliary information. While you're chatting, I can just open up a web browser. If they say something or talk about an event that happened, I can just immediately look it up on Google, get up to speed, and then reply to them. Whereas when I'm talking in those little group discussions, one of the group members might say something and I don't really know anything about it, but I also don't have the resources to go and look it up real quick.

Although this type of information gathering occurred moderately frequently, there was only one case where there was evidence that students used the Internet to gather substantive information about the argument. In the face-to-face classroom, I never observed this type of search for additional information because the students did not have their computers available.

Sometimes, however, students in the online environment focused on irrelevant outside activities, such as making lunch:

1. **Jonathan:** it seems that mr Ben is M.I.A.
2. **Jonathan:** or we can no longer see his text
3. **Ben:** sorry
4. **Ben:** was making a sandwich
5. **Jonathan:** haha
6. **Ben:** didn't think you would notice
7. **Carlos:** hey i made a sandwich too
8. **Carlos:** that's the best part of doing this stuff online

In this particular discussion, three of the students make references to leaving their computers to make lunch during the discussion. In other online conversations, there is evidence that students were playing online games or reading email. This behavior probably occurs because it is easy to "walk away" from a discussion for a brief period online without being noticed.

For a number of reasons—some good and some bad—conversations in the online environment seem to take a little more than twice the time than do comparable conversations in the face-to-face classroom. Although further research is needed to determine the applicability of this factor (i.e., 2x) to other conversational domains, it seems likely that online conversations will always require more time than face-to-face conversations because (1) typing takes more time than oral speech and (2) there is an amount of lag in the chat system that allows participants to split their attention to other tasks.

4.4.4 Complicating Factors

This study attempted to control for a number of complicating factors, such as the topic of discussion and, to a lesser degree, learning effects. However, this study still took place in a naturalistic setting and has many of the complicating factors that go along with such a setting (Brown, 1992). Most notably, the instructor participated in some of the classroom discussions, but not in any of the online conversations. In the classroom, Ed behaved as he normally does; he wandered from group to group provoking the students to think about the issues as he saw fit. Typically, Ed stayed with one group for about five or ten minutes, which meant that he rarely made it to all groups before the discussions were over. In the online environment, however, he had no interaction with the students. There is some evidence that the groups interacting with Ed in the classroom (mean = 0.39; st.dev = 0.83) performed better than those that did not interact with him (mean = 0.05; st.dev = 0.94), but the difference is not significant ($p = 0.51$ using a two-tailed T-test assuming equal variance). Although the portions of the discussion involving Ed were usually productive, he only participated in three of the fourteen face-to-face discussions and none of the online conversations.

The size of the groups was a second partially controlled variable. Although all students were assigned to four-person groups, not every student attended every class. Out of the twenty-five discussions, ten began with all four students. The fourth student arrived late in three additional discussions. Another ten discussions included only three of the four students, and two discussions included only two students. In general, three person groups (mean = 0.21; st.dev = 1.01) might perform a little better than four person groups (mean = –0.10; st.dev = 0.92), but the difference is not significant (p = 0.45 using a two-tailed T-test assuming equal variance). In the two person groups, one performed fairly well while the other performed relatively poorly. Further research is needed to understand the factors that lead to the observed differences between groups.

4.5 SUMMARY

In this chapter, I have presented a quasi-experimental study that examined how the quality of discussion content varied between the face-to-face classroom and the online chatroom. The results show that the quality of the chat-based conversations was comparable to those in the face-to-face environment. However, there was wide variance between the discussions, which suggests that more research is needed on group dynamics in this setting. The data also show that efficiency is diminished; achieving quality discussions online requires significantly more time. This reduction in efficiency seems to be caused by both the inherent difficulty of conveying complex ideas in text, and the splitting of attention that chatrooms enable. In the next chapter, I consider the design implications of these findings and of the findings presented in the previous chapter.

CHAPTER 5

DESIGNING BETTER ONLINE LEARNING ENVIRONMENTS

5.1 THE CHALLENGE OF ONLINE LEARNING

Social settings have certain affordances that help us know how we should behave (Goffman, 1959, 1963). The physical environment of the church, for example, suggests a quiet, respectful demeanor while a bar encourages boisterous behavior. Some people miss these social cues, but most of us are quite adept at interpreting them and behaving appropriately in various physical settings. In online environments, the social cues may be different, but they still operate to shape behavior (Wallace, 1999; Joinson, 2003). These changing social affordances, however, make it difficult to take traditional pedagogical approaches and simply use them, as they are, in online media (Bruckman, 1999). In moving into online learning, we need to understand how these social mechanisms influence learning behaviors.

In this book, I have focused on one particularly interesting medium: text-based chat. I have described how media choice (i.e., chat versus face-to-face) influences the process and content of small group discussions among college students. Joinson (2003) points out, however, that media effects cannot simply be assumed. Although features of different media can promote different behaviors, we are not passive media consumers. Instead, we often consciously choose between media to support certain types of interaction or even appropriate old media for new uses. In the next section, I review the findings from this research with an eye toward conscious, specific design decisions that we can make when designing educational environments. Then, I pull up to a higher level and consider some of the more general implications for theory and design.

5.2 KEY FINDINGS OF THIS RESEARCH

Throughout this book, I have focused on how the choice between using face-to-face and chat environments affects educational discussions among small groups of college students. I have presented two studies that looked at the quality of the discussion process (Chapter 3) and of the discussion content (Chapter 4). The first study used a case study approach to describe the ways that chat environments influence the discussion process in foreign language learning environments. Although the instructors in this learning domain prepared specific discussion topics each day, they were not concerned if discussions veered off-topic. As long as students actively used their foreign language, these instructors were pleased. Therefore, this study was concerned with the process of having a discussion online, and did not focus on the content of the discussion. In order to examine the quality of the discussion content, I conducted a second study in a different learning domain—professional ethics education. This quasi-experimental study focused on the content of small group discussions in the chat environment compared with face-to-face conversations on the same topics. Through examining both discussion process and discussion content in educational chat environments, I have shown three things:

1. Properties of the chat medium seem to discourage conversational dominance by any one individual through (a) denying that individual mechanisms to control the conversational floor and (b) reducing the inhibition felt by shy or otherwise disempowered students.
2. The choice of medium does not seem to affect the quality of discussion content nearly as much as other variables.
3. Efficiency is diminished in chatrooms; achieving quality discussions online requires significantly more time because (a) typing is slower than speaking and

(b) students are able to take part in parallel activities while engaging in a chat discussion.

Below, I review each of these findings in more detail.

5.2.1 Conversational Dominance

In foreign language learning, there is ample evidence to suggest that chat environments lead to a reduction in power dominance with little, if any, impact on language production skills (Kelm, 1992; Kern, 1995; Beauvois, 1997; Warschauer, 1997). There is even some evidence to suggest that interaction in text-based, chat environments can help improve oral language skills (Payne & Whitney, 2002; Payne & Ross, 2005). As Ortega (1997) points out, however, it is important to develop a deeper understanding of how and why this online medium encourages these behavioral changes.

In Chapter 3, I have suggested one model that builds on previous work on disinhibition online (Prentice-Dunn & Rogers, 1982; Kiesler, Siegel, & McGuire, 1984; Sproull & Kiesler, 1991; Joinson, 1998; Wallace, 1999; Spears, Lea, & Postmes, 2001; Joinson, 2003) to provide a way of looking at the complicated interaction of four factors affecting learning behavior. Based on the bystander effect (i.e., Latané & Darley, 1970), a social-psychological theory of the causes of inhibition in emergency situations, this model suggests that four social psychological mechanisms (and their interactions) deserve careful attention in the design and analysis of online learning environments: self-awareness, social cues, diffusion of responsibility, and blocking.

Understanding how these four social psychological mechanisms highlighted by the bystander effect contribute to or reduce dominance can help us see some ways to avoid dominance in the design of new online learning environments. For example, social facilitation theory (Zajonc, 1965; Baumeister, 1984; Geen, 1991) suggests that low-confidence students benefit the most from environments that reduce self-awareness, which can occur when an interface focuses attention on identification with group goals and norms (Lea & Spears, 1991; Postmes & Spears, 1998; Spears, Lea, & Postmes, 2001) or when it focuses attention away from the perception of an audience (Baumeister, 1984; Matheson & Zanna, 1988; Joinson, 2001b).

This analysis also suggested that reducing certain social cues that students unintentionally give off can increase participation, particularly among low-confidence students. Being able to work through mistakes privately (e.g., correct misspelled words or look up words in the dictionary) before expressing ideas to peers helped students to feel more comfortable in the online environment. This suggests that the integration of tools to privately identify and correct mistakes might further improve participation among low-confidence students. For example, in foreign language learning, a chat interface that identifies misspelled words (similar to the interface in many text editors) could promote greater reflection over mistakes while simultaneously encouraging more equitable participation.

The lack of blocking in chat environments played an important role in relaxing time pressures in the online environment. Given that all students could type comments simultaneously, students did not feel the pressure of holding up the class as they struggled to write down their ideas. Many authors have worried that this creates new threading structures that hinder comprehension (e.g., Werry, 1996; M. Smith, Cadiz, & Burkhalter, 2002), but no students mentioned this as a problem in either learning domain studied in this book. In fact, Herring's (1999) analysis of interactional coherence in chat suggests that this is an easily understood new form of linguistic play. It is worth noting, however, that chat participants sometimes still attempt to introduce mechanisms to control the conversational floor, even when blocking is not possible (Simpson, 2005). Further research is needed to examine how interface decisions—for example, indications of when someone begins typing in IM clients—can affect blocking and the resulting dominance of educational conversations.

Finally, a theoretical analysis based on the social psychological literature indicated that diffusion of responsibility plays a role in influencing participation patterns, although I did not observe this in my experimental setup. Certainly, diffusion of responsibility can be affected by pedagogical decisions, but it can also be influenced by interface design. In the section on efficiency of conversation below, I describe in more detail some research on social proxies (Erickson & Kellogg, 2000; Erickson, Halverson, Kellogg, Laff, & Wolf, 2002; DiMicco, Pandolfo, & Bender, 2004) that have been used to increase individual feelings of responsibility and encourage more equitable participation.

5.2.2 Quality of Discussion Content

In working with foreign language learning, I examined the discussion process and showed that chat environments help to promote greater interaction and reduced power structures, which thrilled the course instructors, who were not overly concerned with the content of these discussions. It is also important, however, to understand how these changes in inhibition affect the content of the discussion. In talking more, do online students still make relevant contributions? To answer this question, I focused on the use of chat discussions in a professional ethics class in computer science.

Chapter 4 described a quasi-experimental study designed to assess the relative quality of discussion content in chat and face-to-face environments. In order to compare the quality of discussion content on an open-ended topic, I developed a coding metric that aggregated ideas across all groups to create an "ideal" conversation. Group scores were based on how well an individual discussion conformed to this aggregated list of ideas. By comparing group scores in face-to-face and chat-based discussions on the same topics, I showed that variation between and within groups overshadowed any differences that might have existed between media. Although I found no statistically significant differences between the quality of face-to-face conversations and conversations in the chatrooms, there is a great amount of variation from one group to the next, which raises questions for future work.

Where exactly does this variance come from? Informal analysis of the discussions in this study suggests that there are a number of factors that might be important sources of variance. For example, Group 2, which typically scored relatively high, involved one student who had previous formal ethical training and liked to play the role of devil's advocate. This student often provoked the other students by taking an intentionally conflicting position. In doing this, he forced the others to better defend their own positions and to critically engage a viewpoint they might have otherwise ignored. He also used his formal ethical training to highlight some of the deeper ethical issues in clear language. It is possible that other groups implicitly discussed some of these same issues but were never able to articulate them. The high-scoring group discussions often seemed to be marked by the greatest amount of conflict.

Another possible explanation returns to the social loafing literature. As I discussed in Chapter 3, a body of literature known as *social loafing* emerged out of the work on the bystander effect. Social loafing researchers explicitly asked questions about motivation to participate in group situations. In particular, Karau and Williams (1993) argue that three factors seem to play an important role in influencing individual motivation to pursue group goals: (1) the belief that high effort will lead to a valued outcome (known as *expectancy*), (2) the degree to which an individual feels that he or she is instrumental to obtaining that outcome (known as *instrumentality*), and (3) the degree to which the outcome is viewed as desirable (known as *valence*). In fact, Karau and Williams explicitly define the combination of these three variables—expectancy, instrumentality, and valence—as the "motivational force" (p. 685) acting on an individual in a group setting. Given explanatory power of social loafing for describing differences of effort in group tasks (e.g., Geen, 1991; Karau & Williams, 1993), it is quite possible that these factors contributed significantly to the amount of variation in quality observed in this study. Further research is needed to better understand these potential explanations of the variance observed.

5.2.3 Efficiency of Conversational Medium
The results from this analysis suggest that the conversational medium has relatively little impact on the discussion content compared with other factors. However, the data also suggest that conversations in chatrooms require more time to cover the same material. Students need longer in the online environment, in part because typed discussions occur at a slower pace, but also because students seem to divide their attention between the chat discussion and other activities.

This suggests that one of the biggest changes to occur when educational discussions move from the face-to-face classroom to a chat environment is not quality, but rather efficiency and pacing. To achieve the same results as a face-to-face group, an online group seems to simply need more time. This is not necessarily a problem, but interface design can likely play a role in altering pacing in the online environment. For example, it is possible that the addition of *social translucence* tools—interfaces that make social behavior such as participation or non-participation more visible—would encourage greater attention to the conversation at hand. In Erickson and Kellogg's work on social proxies, they have found that adding a simple diagram that shows the time since each interlocutor last participated can have a impact on the flow of conversation in a chat environment (Erickson & Kellogg, 2000; Erickson, Halverson, Kellogg, Laff, & Wolf, 2002). In fact, they suggest that peer pressure on unresponsive group members contributes to these new conversational dynamics. DiMicco (2004) developed a similar tool for face-to-face settings, which also seems to encourage positive peer pressure on both quiet and talkative individuals.

5.3 ON SYNCHRONICITY

Before moving on to future work, it is useful to briefly consider some of the higher-level implications for our understanding of computer-mediated communication (CMC). The research literature traditionally refers to chat as a *synchronous* CMC technology. As this research has shown, however, the binary distinction between synchronous and asynchronous technologies is something of a misnomer. It is true that chat technologies typically require all interlocutors to be simultaneously logged into the online environment, but the resulting discussions are not truly synchronous. Unlike face-to-face environments, members of a chatroom are socially able to take some time to compose their thoughts in private before presenting them as "complete" expressions. In other words, there is a small amount of lag in chat environments, which seems to play an important role in creating new conversational patterns.

In Chapter 3, I described a number of ways that this lag contributed to reducing student inhibition in a foreign language learning environment. Students did not feel put on the spot when asked a question. They did not feel as if they were holding anyone else up when they struggled to present their ideas. They felt more comfortable about being able to correct some of their mistakes before making them public. In Chapter 4, I described how the lag gives students in a professional ethics environment a little additional time to do other important activities, such as looking up additional information, composing their thoughts on a new idea, or even making a sandwich.

Although we often talk about the binary distinction between synchronous and asynchronous environments, this work emphasizes that synchronicity is a continuum. The timing of interaction in a classroom has much in common with the timing of conversation online, but there are important differences. Chat discussions are not as synchronous as face-to-face conversations; the level of immediacy is diminished in the chat environment. This difference in synchronicity—that is, the lag introduced in the chat environment—appears to have important implications for the resulting conversational dynamics.

5.4 IMPLICATIONS FOR DESIGNERS

In addition to the specific design suggestions that arose out of the bystander effect, the lag in chat environments is an important feature that might be worth introducing into other technologies. I have described how the temporal rhythms of chatrooms are somewhat different from the rhythms of face-to-face discussion. In the chatroom, there is a small amount of lag during which students can do other things. They can take a few extra seconds to compose their thoughts or simply to check email. This small amount of delay seems to play an important role in many of the changes that were observed in these studies.

This suggests that it might be useful to intentionally build online learning environments that have a certain amount of lag. For a variety of reasons, students in face-to-face environments often feel as if they do not have the time that they need to compose their thoughts. Introducing lag into an online learning environment removes the social pressure to respond immediately. This, in turn, gives some students the thinking time that they need in order to feel comfortable as an active participant in the discussion.

Increased lag time, however, also enables negative social behaviors. The social pressures that inhibit students in the classroom are the same pressures that encourage them to arrive on time and to remain focused on the educational material. In both of the studies described here (and the pilot studies that led up to them), students arrived late to the online sessions more frequently than they did to the classroom face-to-face discussions. Likewise, Chapter 4 described evidence of students splitting their attention between the topic(s) under discussion and other activities, which they would never do in the face-to-face classroom. In reducing inhibition, the chatroom environment enabled many educationally productive social behaviors, but it also enabled some less desirable ones.

In designing online learning environments, it is important for designers to keep these trade-offs in mind. No environment is perfect; there are always advantages and disadvantages. Through being aware of the disadvantages, however, we can develop environments and pedagogical practices to best protect against them.

5.5 FUTURE DIRECTIONS

Face-to-face environments have a number of unique advantages that we have not been able to—and, perhaps, cannot—replicate in CMC tools (Kiesler & Cummings, 2002; Kraut, Fussell, Brennan, & Siegel, 2002; Nardi & Whittaker, 2002; Olson, Teasley, Covi, & Olson, 2002). However, CMC tools also have a number of unique advantages over face-to-face interaction, such as reduced power hierarchies (Kiesler, Siegel, & McGuire, 1984; Dubrovsky, Kiesler, & Sethna, 1991; Sproull & Kiesler, 1991) and increased willingness to share personal viewpoints (Weisband & Kiesler, 1996; Joinson, 2001a, 2001b). It is important to be able to design online learning environments to support education at a distance, but it is also important to understand how these same environments may supplement traditional, face-to-face instruction. Ultimately, we want to be able to knowledgably choose between various communication media to best support the desired interaction. The question remains, however, what type of communication environment is most appropriate for a given purpose?

Although this work provides insight into the use of chatrooms to support educational discussions, it is only one small piece of this larger question. In my studies, I have investigated the use of chatrooms to support educational discussions in a fairly narrow set of conditions. All of my research involved students who knew one another from face-to-face settings, students who had significant experience with computer technology, and open-ended (i.e., conjunctive) discussion topics. In designing effective online environments, however, we know that other variables, such as moderation (Collison, Elbaum, Haavind, & Tinker, 2000) and relationship building (Walther, 1996; Haythornthwaite, 2002; Haythornthwaite & Kazmer, 2004) also play important roles. How might issues of moderation affect these findings, especially the quality and efficiency of discussion? Might more careful team-building activities affect relationships, particularly with concern to power and dominance?

Not only do questions remain about chat environments, but it is also an open question of how well these findings can generalize to other CMC media. How might these same issues of quality and efficiency play out in other CMC environments, such as, for example, threaded discussion spaces? Which types of problems and activities are best suited for chat versus other media? What is the appropriate balance between using chat environments and using other media?

We must be careful, however, in how we approach these questions. To date, research on the effectiveness of online learning has been described as a "methodological morass" (Bernard, Abrami, Lou, & Borokhovski, 2004). Some studies have found that online learning environments improve learning, while others have found that they reduce learning (Lou, Abrami, & d'Apollonia, 2001; Bernard et al., 2004). Few of these studies, however, systematically pull apart, or even describe, the influence of various media and pedagogical choices (Bernard, Abrami, Lou, & Borokhovski, 2004), which makes it difficult to draw any conclusions. To move forward, we need to begin separating the various, complicated variables that affect learning behaviors. I have shown some of the ways media can influence learning behaviors. Learning, however, is the result of complicated interactions between these behaviors and a number of other factors, which we are only beginning to understand.

APPENDIX A

DISCUSSION TOPICS AND AGGREGATED ANSWERS

A.1 PRIVACY AND BLOGS (DAY 1)

I want you to think about the following scenario in class (based on a true story) and discuss the questions that follow. Spend roughly the same amount of time on each of the questions so that you get to discuss them all.

A friend of mine, "Carol," has two college-aged children, "Alice" and "Bob" who are attending universities several hundred miles away from Atlanta. Both have blogs that they use as personal journals and to communicate with their friends. Neither of them has told Carol about their blog or given her the URL. Carol, however, knows one of the handles that Bob often uses for IM and game accounts, and using this knowledge and search engines has discovered Bob's blog. Bob's blogging software provides a "friend" feature that allows him to link to other people's blogs, home pages etc., and through Bob's friends list, Carol has also found Alice's blog. Carol thinks that reading Alice and Bob's personal accounts on their blogs is a kind of snooping, but being a caring parent can't resist using her new-found knowledge to check up on how Alice and Bob are doing. What she discovers worries her. While Alice and Bob are both doing okay in college, and neither blog contains accounts of drinking, drugs, or sex, Alice several times mentions her growing interest in skydiving. She says that she knows her parents would object, because of the danger, but she's just really intrigued by the idea of jumping out of a plane and floating there in mid-air. There's a university club that supports the activity and provides all the training and equipment. Some of her friends are into it. She thinks she's going to go for it. Bob, either because he too has been reading Alice's blog or because they stay in touch by email and IM, has found out about this. He doesn't disapprove, but he posts on his blog that he worried that his parents would hate the idea. However, Alice is a big girl now, and he says that it's up to her to tell their parents or not. He's not going to. (Except, indirectly, through Carol discovering his blog first and reading it, he has.)

1. (20 points) How private should people regard information that they post to blogs? Alice and Bob did not advertise their blogs widely in the same way that their e-mail addresses. Should they assume that people they don't expect to know about their blogs are reading what they write?

Perspective	Evidence
• (5 points) Bloggers have no right to expect privacy.	• (0.83 points) Online material that is accessible by anyone on the Internet is public by definition

- (0.83 points) Google search makes things like blogs easily accessible to anyone

- (0.83 points) Posting online requires an explicit action to make information public

- (0.83 points) There are social ways to signify an expectation of privacy (e.g., disclaimers, "keep out" signs, pseudonyms)

- (0.83 points) Online content has an explicit expectation of readership

- (0.83 points) Pseudonyms do not reveal identity to strangers, but identity is easy to figure out with some knowledge about the person (e.g., people use pseudonyms in multiple places, links between friends' blogs can reveal identity)

- (5 points) Bloggers can have a reasonable expectation of privacy in some cases

- (1.67 points) Giving the blog URL to only a few people is a social mechanism for maintaining privacy

- (1.67 points) Anonymity/pseudonymity shows a desire to use social solutions to maintain privacy

- (1.67 points) The psychological properties of the
  medium lead people to
  behave differently than
  they otherwise would

2. (20 points) Carol feels that what she's doing isn't quite
   right, but even if she resolves not to read Alice and
   Bob's blogs again, she already knows what she has
   found out. If she confronts Alice, she will probably get
   her own way, but she will have had to reveal what she
   has been doing. Do Alice and Bob have a right to privacy on their blogs? Is what Carol is doing snooping?
   Is it any different from rifling through their rooms if
   they lived at home to read their personal journals?

Perspective	Evidence
• (2 points) Carol is snooping on her daughter	• (0.67 points) If Carol's intention is to find out information her daughter hasn't told her, then this is snooping • (0.67 points) Based on the Golden Rule, it's wrong to explicitly search for information about other people online • (0.67 points) The relationship of mother/daughter prohib-its reading the journal, no matter the location
• (2 points) Carol's relationship with Alice creates an ethical	• (0.5 points) People without a personal relationship may

obligation to tell her daughter that she has found out about and read the blog

read a blog without informing the blogger, but those who might have an impact on the blogger's life must tell her

- (0.5 points) If Carol tells Alice about reading the blog, Alice will have the opportunity to take appropriate corrective action (e.g., restricting readers, taking down the blog)

- (0.5 points) Not telling is essentially lying

- (0.5 points) Reading a blog once because of accidentally finding it is acceptable

- (2 points) Reading a blog is not like reading a journal

- (0.33 points) A blog is similar to a journal that's been posted in a public place (e.g., a bulletin board)

- (0.33 points) A digital equivalent of a journal would be one on a PC, not one on the Internet

- (0.33 points) Unlike blogs, journals carry a social expectation of privacy

- (0.33 points) Blogs have an explicit expectation of readership

- (0.33 points) People take specific actions to protect a

Perspective	Evidence
	journal and keep it private (e.g., hide it under a bed, lock it up)
	• (0.33 points) Bedrooms have limited physical access, which engenders an expectation of privacy based on location
• (2 points) Carol is not snooping	• (1 point) Blogs are public forms of communication
	• (1 point) Parents have a responsibility to look out for their children and to protect them
• (4 points) The relationship between Carol and Alice is irrelevant to the ethical considerations about reading the blog	None given

3. (5 points) Can you relate to this on a personal level? How would you feel in Alice's or Bob's situation? Are there things that you want to "publish" within your circle of friends that you maybe don't want your parents to know about?

Perspective	Evidence
• (1.25 points) Cannot relate to the scenario	• (0.42 points) I don't post anything online that shouldn't be shared with everyone
	• (0.42 points) I have no major secrets from my parents or anyone else

	• (0.42 points) I don't have a blog
• (1.25 points) Can relate to the scenario	• (0.42 points) I have information that friends know, but that shouldn't be shared with my parents
	• (0.42 points) I carefully manage my IM away messages so that my parents do not see inappropriate messages
	• (0.42 points) I know friends who do not carefully manage their blogs

4. (10 points) What if Alice were not contemplating going skydiving but, say dropping out of college? Joining a cult? Having a sex change operation? What if she or Bob described wild orgies, run-ins with the police, the fact they were on academic probation? Would the significance of the information they reveal (the ends) justify Carol's actions (the means)?

Perspective	Evidence
• (1.67 points) The content of blogs is irrelevant to ethical considerations about reading them	• (0.83 points) Blogs are public • (0.83 points) Serious events (e.g., suicidal tendencies) would morally demand intervention by anyone, not just a parent
• (1.67 points) Content makes a difference	• (1.67 points) Serious events (e.g., suicidal-tendencies) would morally

	demand intervention by anyone, not just a parent
• (3.33 points) For a parent, there is a difficult balance between protecting your children and respecting their freedoms and privacy	None given

5. (5 points) Alice is 21 years old. What if, like Bob, she were 19? What if she was 25 and at grad school?

Perspective	Evidence
• (1.25 points) Age is irrelevant	• (1.25 points) The age of a blogger has no impact on the ethical considerations of reading the blog
• (1.25 points) Age is relevant, but only for minors	• (0.75 points) Minors have a reduced right to privacy because the consequences of actions may be different than they are for adults
	• (0.75 points) Minors talking about illegal behavior (i.e., drinking) in a blog is a problem

6. (30 points) What if Alice and Bob were Carol's employees, not her children, and Alice's personal blog said that she was dissatisfied at work and was considering a job offer from a competitor? There are cases of people having been fired in situations like this. Is that fair/reasonable?

Perspective	Evidence
• (1.88 points) Employers have a right to read employees' public blogs	• (0.94 points) Blogs are public • (0.94 points) Blogs have technical means for obtaining privacy (e.g., passwords)
• (1.88 points) Ethically, there is a difference between stumbling across an employee's blog and searching for it	• (0.94 points) Stumbling across a blog is like overhearing/overseeing something in public • (0.94 points) Employers should not actively seek to intrude into employees' personal lives
• (1.88 points) Employers can fire an employee over the content of a personal blog	• (0.38 points) Employers have fired employees over blogs in the real world (e.g., Dooce.com) • (0.38 points) Employers have a right to fire anyone for any reason • (0.38 points) Employers have an obligation to ensure that one employee does not create a negative work environment • (0.38 points) Employers have a right/obligation to protect the company's image/reputation • (0.38 points) Employers have a right to restrict

employees' free speech
rights as it pertains to the
company

• (1.88 points) Employers should not fire an employee over comments made on a personal blog	• (0.31 points) Dissent in/ about the workplace should be encouraged, not stifled
	• (0.31 points) Employers can never restrict personal rights and liberties, such as free speech
	• (0.31 points) Employers should respect the separation between work and personal life
	• (0.31 points) Firing someone for comments made on a personal blog degrades trust in the workplace
	• (0.31 points) Web forums are designed to be environments for free exploration of identity without consequences
	• (0.31 points) Firing someone for comments made on a blog treats them merely as a means, violating the principles of deontological ethics
• (1.88 points) The consequences should be proportional to the action	• (0.23 points) Employees may be fired for poor job performance

- (0.23 points) Employees may be disciplined if they disparage the company while acting as a representative of that company

- (0.23 points) Employees may be disciplined if they disparage the company while claiming to act as a representative of that company

- (0.23 points) Employees may be disciplined if they disparage the company while perceived to act as a representative of that company

- (0.23 points) Employers may respond appropriately to illegal action by an employee

- (0.23 points) Employers should consider whether or not employee complaints have merit

- (0.23 points) Employers cannot fire someone for considering another job with a different company

- (0.23 points) Employer responses should be in keeping with company policy

- (1.88 points) Ethical and legal issues are not the same

  - (0.47 points) There are not legal means for enforcing certain ethical stances (e.g., there is no way of enforcing the stance that it's ok to accidentally discover a blog, but not to search for it)

  - (0.47 points) Corporations tend to only follow legal obligations, not ethical ones

  - (0.47 points) Sometimes legal protections may hurt a company (e.g., not firing pregnant women), but they are ethically necessary

  - (0.47 points) U.S. law differs from other countries' laws because of different ethical stances on issues

- (1.88 points) The legal/social/ethical landscape with new technologies is often unclear

  - (0.63 points) Legal precedents are difficult to predict

  - (0.63 points) Companies rarely have explicit policies these days that deal with things like personal blogs

  - (0.63 points) Analogies about new technologies (e.g., looking at a blog is like looking in a window) fail because new technologies do not necessarily have the same legal protections as the analogy suggests.

- (3.75 points) Ethical issues   None given
  are difficult to decide
  in the abstract

A.2 EMPLOYEES ACCESSING PRIVATE INFORMATION (DAY 2)

Last time, we looked at a scenario concerning privacy and blogs. The main issue that arose in discussion was whether the protagonists had a reasonable expectation of privacy, and most of you said that they were naive in assuming that anything posted without password protection would be secret. This brought up the differences in opinions and expectations between technically knowledgeable people, such as information technology professionals, and the general public.

Today, you're going to discuss a couple of scenarios in which the role of computing professionals, not the general public, are more central. Spend a couple of minutes thinking about the scenarios on your own, and then discuss in your group each of the questions that follow. There are two scenarios, and seven (five plus two) questions. Give approximately equal time to discussing each of the questions, so that you finish the exercise.

A.2.1 Scenario 1

You work for a company that maintains a large database of personal information about members of the public. The content of the database is the company's intellectual property. Someone approaches you and asks for a copy of a person's file. He will pay you $1,000.

1. (5 points) Who is affected by your decision?

Perspective	Evidence/Logical Support
• (0.36 points) You are affected	• (0.36 points) You might be punished for your actions (e.g., get fired, be sued)
• (0.36 points) The company is affected	• (0.12 points) The information is the company's property
	• (0.12 points) The company should be making money off of the information
	• (0.12 points) Selling the information might cause the company to lose future customers
• (0.71 points) The target of the information request is affected	None given
• (0.71 points) The person requesting the information is affected	None given
• (0.36 points) The other people in the database are affected	• (0.36 points) Slippery slope argument: If you sell one, what's to stop you from selling the next one?
• (0.36 points) The other employees at the company are affected	• (0.36 points) Selling the information might cause a public scandal, which would hurt the company's reputation and, by extension, the other employees' reputations

- (0.71 points) The people   None given
  that you might spend the
  money on (e.g., your
  family) are affected

---

2. (15 points) What are some alternative courses of action
that you might follow?

Perspective	Evidence
• (1.07 points) Ignore the request, and pretend like it never happened	• (1.07 points) Talking about the incident might violate the privacy of the requester
• (1.07 points) Just say "no"	• (1.07 points) The personal risk is high and there is no guarantee that you can trust the requester
• (1.07 points) Sell the information	• (1.07 points) The target may not mind if he/she is given a share of the money
• (1.07 points) Sell false information	• (1.07 points) Problem: This might put you in danger
• (1.07 points) Tell the police	• (1.07 points) If you tell the target, you should tell the police as well
• (1.07 points) Don't tell the police	• (0.54 points) This should be the target's decision, not yours • (0.54 points) If you don't sell the information, no illegal action has actually occurred

- (1.07 points) Report the incident to the company and follow company policy

- (0.15 points) Company policy probably requires reporting

- (0.15 points) The company's official representatives should take any action, not you as an individual employee

- (0.15 points) The company owns the data

- (0.15 points) The company probably has a security team set up and trained for this type of thing

- (0.15 points) Just in case something happens in the future/Secrecy always leads to problems

- (0.15 points) If the company is aware of the incident, it can be more vigilant about watching the target's record for suspicious behavior from other employees

- (0.15 points) You should follow company policy unless it seems unethical or personally unacceptable

---

3. (25 points – Combined with Q4[27]) One possible action would be to contact the person whose information is being sought and tell him or her of the incident. Is this

action ethically prohibited, obligatory or neither? If neither, what factors would point toward telling the person, and what would point toward not doing so?

Perspective	Evidence
• (3.13 points) You should tell the target of the information request	• (0.45 points) The Golden Rule: I would want to know if someone tried to get my information, so I should tell the target person
	• (0.45 points) If you tell other external parties (e.g., the police), you should also tell the target person
	• (0.45 points) Some laws require divulging the request if personal information has been unintentionally released
	• (0.45 points) Telling the target person is important to maintaining their relationship with the company
	• (0.45 points) It's a nice gesture
	• (0.45 points) There is no reason not to tell the target
	• (0.45 points) It's not ethically wrong to tell the target person
• (3.13 points) You should not tell the target of the information request	• (0.45 points) It's not ethically required to contact the target person

- (0.45 points) The Golden Rule: I would not want to know every time someone asked for my information, so I shouldn't tell the target person

- (0.45 points) No information has been divulged, so no harm occurred

- (0.45 points) Telling the target person might put someone else (e.g., the requester of the information) in danger

- (0.45 points) Telling the target person will cause them unnecessary worry

- (0.45 points) Handling the situation internally avoids big problems

- (0.45 points) There's nothing that the target person can do about it anyway

- (3.13 points) Attenuating circumstances could change the situation

- (1.04 points) The sensitive of the information requested (e.g., grocery lists versus credit history) may influence the decision

- (1.04 points) The source of the request (e.g., government agency versus the mob) may influence the decision

- (1.04 points) The potential for danger to the target

	person may influence the decision
• (3.13 points) There are potentially conflicting ethical obligations in this scenario	• (1.04 points) The company policy may be in conflict with the ethically correct course of action
	• (1.04 points) There is a tension between your obligation to inform the target person and your obligation not to unnecessarily worry the target person
	• (1.04 points) The ethics and laws governing a situ-ation are often different

4. (25 points – Combined with Q3) Explain which one of the actions (either one of yours from your answer to (b), or the action suggested in (c)) you should choose in preference to the others.

5. (20 points) Now consider a variation of this scenario: You find out that another employee is selling personal information. What actions are open to you in this scenario? On balance, what should you do?

Perspective	Evidence
• (2.00 points) Report the other employee to the company and follow company policy	• (0.40 points) The company may reward you for this behavior
	• (0.40 points) The data belongs to the company

• (0.40 points) Since the employee has sold information, there's the potential for large problems like lawsuits	
• (0.40 points) The company can appropriately punish the individual (e.g., fire them, sue them)	
• (0.40 points) You should follow company policy as long as it isn't personally unacceptable	
• (4.00 points) Call the police	None given
• (2.00 points) Blackmail the other employee	• (2.00 points) The other employee has no recourse against you
• (4.00 points) Confront the other employee	None given
• (4.00 points) Ignore the other employee's actions	None given

A.2.2 Scenario 2

Some IRS employees are authorized to obtain credit reports from credit bureaus for official use by the agency. The IRS has found a significant number of cases where employees have illegally accessed people's credit reports for their own purposes.

6. (25 points) Suggest some procedural measures that would reduce this problem and suggest reasonable penalties. As a consultant setting up the system that accesses

credit reports, what advice would you give the IRS management? Or is it their problem to solve?

Perspective	Evidence
• (1.56 points) Log everything that happens on the system	• (0.78 points) Logging actions provides accountability commensurate with the authority to access this information
	• (0.78 points) Logs allow audits that can look for suspicious behavior
• (1.56 points) Require some sort of approval of all requests for information (e.g., from a peer, from management)	• (1.56 points) This introduces a system of checks and balances
• (3.13 points) Allow employees to access only the minimum amount of identifiable information that they need to do their jobs	None given
• (1.56 points) Require all requests for information to contain an attached written justification	• (0.78 points) Written justifications can be audited to look for suspicious behavior
	• (0.78 points) Lying on a written explanation is documented incriminating evidence if a problem ever arises
• (1.56 points) Maintain a record of information requests connected with	• (0.78 points) Since case files should have an associated profile of

open case files

common information requests, a computer could easily flag information requests that seem unusual

- (0.78 points) Reports can be audited to look for suspicious behavior

- (1.56 points) Enact severe penalties for inappropriately accessing information (e.g., fire the employee, sue them, begin criminal proceedings)

- (0.78 points) High penalties discourage breaking rules

- (0.78 points) High penalties send a strong message that inappropriately accessing information is a serious offense

- (1.56 points) Publish or otherwise harm the credit information of any offender

- (1.56 points) This is similar to city and state laws that post information about convicted sex offenders

- (1.56 points) Any of these solutions have a number of limitations

- (0.52 points) Any solution must include a social component, or it will fail

- (0.52 points) Any solution cannot make the work too inefficient

- (0.52 points) Any solution that requires someone to authorize a request should be designed in a way that ensures that approver actively considers each request rather than simply signing off on requests automatically

7. (10 points) As a system designer, in what ways are you responsible for foreseeing these problems and designing in procedural or technical measures to reduce them? Is your job to implement what the customer asks for (assuming that it is legal), or do you have a responsibility sometimes to point out that something that a customer requires may go wrong procedurally because of human/ organizational problems? If you think the IRS example is a bad example of this, what might be a better example?

Perspective	Evidence
• (1.25 points) The consultant is not responsible for foreseeing problems	• (0.42 points) It's simply impossible for one person to foresee all potential problems
	• (0.42 points) There is no ethical obligation to share insights into potential problems
	• (0.42 points) The consultant is only obliged to follow the design specifications given to him/her
• (1.25 points) The consultant has a responsibility for trying to foresee problems	• (0.31 points) By informing the company of potential problems in the beginning, the consultant is not responsible when they actually occur
	• (0.31 points) The ACM Code of Ethics states that, if designers have specialized knowledge, they are obligated to share it

- (0.31 points) Consultants can turn down jobs if they disagree with the company's decisions

- (0.31 points) Architects are required to make buildings structurally sound, even if the specification is not structurally sound

- (1.25 points) The company and the consultant have shared responsibility for identifying problems

- (0.31 points) The solutions to problems are both technical and social, but the consultant/designer can only solve the technical part

- (0.31 points) The design process, which should include both the company and the consultant, should be aimed at identifying potential problems

- (0.31 points) Even if designers raise issues, customers have the final say in how or whether to fix them

- (0.31 points) The level of security should be appropriate to the expected use of the system, which means that systems with little chance of harm do not need to focus too many resources on creating technical solutions

- (1.25 points) Independent of the ethics of the situation suggesting improvements is simply good business practice

- (0.63 points) It's better business to design a better product

- (0.63 points) Getting the software right the first time creates a better customer relationship

A.3 EMPLOYEE MONITORING (DAY 3)

Read the following scenario and then discuss the following five questions. Spend about the same amount of time on each of the questions.

As the information systems manager for a small manufacturing plant, you are responsible for all aspects of the use of information technology. A new inventory control system is being developed to track the quantity and movement of all finished products stored in a local warehouse. Each time a fork-lift operator moves a case of product, he or she must first scan the UPC code on the case. Not only is the product information captured, but also the day, time, and fork-lift operator identification. This data is transmitted over a local-area network to the inventory control computer that then displays information about the case and where it should be placed in the warehouse.

The warehouse manager is excited about using the case movement data for another purpose. It can be used to monitor the productivity of the workers. He will be able to tell how many cases per shift each operator moves, and he plans to use this information to provide performance feedback that could result in pay increases or termination.

[adapted from Reynolds, George "Ethics in Information Technology" Thomson Course Technology, 2003]

1. (35 points – Combined with Q3) The warehouse manager has asked you if there are any potential issues with using the data for recognizing productivity, and, if so, what should be done to avoid them. How would you respond? Think about ethical and legal issues in general, but also how these ethical/legal issues might be influenced by the technical capabilities and limitations of the technology.

Perspective	Evidence
• (7.00 points) Although data monitoring is legal, it might not necessarily be ethical	None given
• (3.50 points) Data monitoring in the workplace is not a problem	• (0.29 points) Data monitoring allows employers to be more objective when making comparisons between employees • (0.29 points) Hard-working employees have nothing to worry about; it's only the lazy employees who must be concerned • (0.29 points) Hard-working employees will benefit from data monitoring • (0.29 points) Workers who don't like being monitored can always find another job elsewhere

- (0.29 points) Workers who
don't like being monitored
can always take action to
make their voices heard
(e.g., join a union)

- (0.29 points) Employers
have a right to know what
their employees are doing
during company time

- (0.29 points) Data monitoring
is no different than having
a manager watch you at all
times

- (0.29 points) Data monitoring
increases efficiency for the
company

- (0.29 points) Monitoring
will allow a company to
punish poor performers

- (0.29 points) Monitoring
has been used in the workplace for quite a while

- (0.29 points) The company
has an obligation to protect
itself from legal liability
that occurs if an employee
misbehaves on the job

- (0.29 points) Data monitoring
can create healthy forms of
competition

- (3.50 points) Data monitoring
in the workplace will create
problems

- (0.39 points) Data
monitoring can create
unhealthy forms of
competition

- (0.39 points) Data monitoring creates additional stress for employees

- (0.39 points) Employees will learn how to manipulate the statistics with their performance

- (0.39 points) Employees simply won't like being monitored

- (0.39 points) Data monitoring will hurt the level of trust in the workplace

- (0.39 points) Since management controls the data, they will be able to manipulate the numbers to say what they want

- (0.39 points) Employees often have tasks that do not lend themselves to easy measurement

- (0.39 points) Employees may not be comfortable with a new technological device or understand how it works

- (0.39 points) Any technological errors in the system affect the employees directly

---

- (3.50 points) There are ways to make employees more

- (0.70 points) Informing workers of the monitoring

comfortable with data monitoring

and how data will be used will make them more comfortable

- (0.70 points) Seeking worker input on data monitoring can make them more comfortable

- (0.70 points) Decisions based on the data should keep in mind extenuating circumstances

- (0.70 points) Using aggregate data (i.e., not singling out individual workers, but looking at general performance of the workplace) would reduce concern

- (0.70 points) Using the data to provide employees with constant feedback about performance would reduce concern

---

- (3.50 points) Other information may be relevant for making ethical decisions

- (0.88 points) There is a difference between using data monitoring to reward good performance and using it to punish bad performance

- (0.88 points) The amount of data collected is relevant to determining the ethics of the situation

- (0.88 points) The social structure and demonstrated

worthiness of trust in the
workplace affects whether
or not data monitoring is
right

- (0.88 points) Intended use
of the data affects whether
or not monitoring is right

2. (15 points) What if the data were used not to reward
productivity but to promote safety? For example, if the
plant were an explosives factory, it might be important
to monitor whether the fork-lift operators were driving
too fast or transferring materials too quickly, as these
could lead to serious hazards to themselves and co-
workers. Would your answer to the previous question
be any different in this situation?

Perspective	Evidence
• (2.50 points) Data monitoring for safety is fine	• (0.50 points) If monitoring productivity data is considered ok, then monitoring to promote safety should be extra ok
	• (0.50 points) Monitoring for safety promotes a better environment that benefits everyone in the workplace
	• (0.50 points) Since workers often fear management reprimands, monitoring should promote a safer environment

- (0.50 points) Management's intentions are ethical when it comes to promoting safety

- (0.50 points) Focusing on safety should improve management relationships with employees because management is seen as more caring

• (2.50 points) Data monitoring for safety might cause problems	• (1.25 points) If management has data about safety, then they are legally liable if anything bad happens
	• (1.25 points) This sends mixed messages to work faster (for productivity) and to work slower (for safety)
• (2.50 points) There are potentially more appropriate ways to accomplish these goals	• (1.25 points) Data should be filtered to only should unsafe behavior so that management cannot also use it to surreptitiously measure productivity
	• (1.25 points) If safety is the issue, other technologies could be used to monitor/ affect speed directly (i.e., speed recorders or physical limits on speed)

3. (35 points – Combined with Q1) If you were a fork-lift operator in either of these scenarios, what would you

be worried about? Do you think that the nature and magnitude of your concerns would be affected by your existing attitudes toward the management of the plant? If so, how and why?

4. (25 points) This previous scenario is about surveillance in the work place. Another safety-related workplace example is the monitoring of long-distance truck drivers to ensure that they take the appropriate number of rests and do not exceed speed limits. Yet another similar example is how car rental companies can monitor the use of their cars by customers. If a customer drives a rental car recklessly or takes it off road, this can now be monitored. Is this any difference from the warehouse or truck company monitoring its employees? Obviously, the customer is not an employee of the rental company, but is the difference between being an employee and being a customer morally relevant?

Perspective	Evidence
• (1.56 points) A trucking company can monitor its drivers	• (0.39 points) Speeding is a real problem with truckers
	• (0.39 points) Truckers are employees of the company
	• (0.39 points) Inaccuracies in the current system for monitoring truckers (i.e., only monitoring when they arrive at certain checkpoints) promotes unsafe behavior

- (0.39 points) Monitoring speed is much less invasive than other technologies currently available (e.g., video or GPS)

- (1.56 points) Monitoring truck drivers may cause problems

- (0.39 points) Monitoring for safety sends mixed messages to drive faster (for productivity) and to drive slower (for safety)

- (0.39 points) Monitoring may upset the drivers, which is bad for business

- (0.39 points) The driver is individually responsible for safety on the road, not the company

- (0.39 points) Monitoring truck drivers rarely works well in practice

- (1.56 points) Monitoring truck drivers is similar to monitoring rental car customers

- (1.56 points) As long as everyone is informed about the monitoring, there is no difference

- (1.56 points) Monitoring truck drivers is different than monitoring rental car customers

- (0.31 points) Truck drivers are employees, not customers

- (0.31 points) Customers have greater flexibility to go elsewhere

- (0.31 points) Truck drivers have more protection from union and federal laws than customers have

- (0.31 points) Employees are informed of policy changes through memos, but customers are rarely explicitly informed of such changes

- (0.31 points) The trucking company is monitoring as a way to improve safety, but the rental car company is not

- (1.56 points) Rental car companies should be free to monitor their customers

- (0.26 points) As long as the customer makes an informed decision, the company can do whatever it wants

- (0.26 points) The customer can always go elsewhere if he/she does not want to be monitored

- (0.26 points) Roughly handling the car does damage, even if it's not visible

- (0.26 points) The car is the company's property

- (0.26 points) Companies have a right to look after their property and protect their investments

- (0.26 points) People rent cars with the intent of destroying them

- (1.56 points) Rental car companies should not monitor their customers

- (0.22 points) Customers have a right to expect a certain degree of privacy

- (0.22 points) If monitoring becomes the industry standard, customers will not have the option of going elsewhere

- (0.22 points) Monitoring leads to rental car companies looking for inappro-priate ways to make a profit (e.g., fees for slightly speeding)

- (0.22 points) Customers do not, and cannot be expected to, read long legalese contracts, which do contain information about monitoring

- (0.22 points) Monitoring customers hurts trust and goodwill, which is necessary for building a business

- (0.22 points) "Damage" done to the car should be physically detectable before charging the customer for it

- (0.22 points) The company already has insurance to cover damage done to cars

• (1.56 points) There are ways of reducing concerns about rental car companies monitoring customers	• (0.39 points) Customers could be given a way to opt out of monitoring
	• (0.39 points) Car companies should only collect information that is highly relevant to protecting cars from damage
	• (0.39 points) Companies should have strict policies on how the collected information is used
	• (0.39 points) Government regulations should restrict how companies announce, collect, and use information
• (3.13 points) Legal and ethical considerations are independent from one another	None given

5. (25 points) Taking the previous question one step further, car manufacturers can also monitor owners. If a customer drives a car in a way discouraged in the car manual, this could void the warranty on, for example, the transmission system or the engine. Data gathered by the car's onboard computer can be uploaded to the manufacturer's computer system when the owner brings the car into the dealer for regular servicing or repairs. Whether the owner has abused the car and voided the warranty can then be determined before repairs take

place. This practice changes the trust relationship that has existed between car owners and dealers. Can you think of any possible problems with this? Is it acceptable?

Perspective	Evidence
• (4.17 points) Manufacturers should be able to monitor customers' driving	• (0.46 points) As long as the customer makes an informed decision, the company can monitor anything it wants
	• (0.46 points) Sensors do not stop the customer from doing anything that he/she wants because the customer does not have to use the warranty
	• (0.46 points) The suggested monitors are much less instructive than alternatives available (e.g., GPS or video)
	• (0.46 points) Rough handling should void the warranty
	• (0.46 points) Some manufacturers have already been doing this for years
	• (0.46 points) Monitoring should lead to decreased maintenance costs, which should be passed on to the customer

- (0.46 points) Customers can always choose to buy from someone else

- (0.46 points) Since the car companies have to pay for warranty repairs, they have a right to make sure that you haven't voided the warranty

- (0.46 points) Car companies can hire someone to follow you around if they want, so why not monitor you?

- (4.17 points) Monitoring customers' cars is a bad idea

- (0.30 points) The customer owns the car, not the manufacturer

- (0.30 points) Although there are no current laws, in the future it may be illegal to remove monitoring devices, like it is currently illegal to mess with the odometer

- (0.30 points) Once monitoring becomes an industry standard, the customer will not be able to go anywhere else

- (0.30 points) This is a slippery slope because some monitoring always leads to more

- (0.30 points) It's impossible to detect when a

problem is with the driving of the car and when the sensor has just gone bad

- (0.30 points) Warranties are necessarily an inexact science

- (0.30 points) Sometimes it's impossible to technologically distinguish between reckless driving and safe, defensive driving

- (0.30 points) Monitoring can lower the level of trust between the customer and the dealer

- (0.30 points) Car manufacturers have all of the control and all of the power in this situation

- (0.30 points) The warnings on the warranty would need to be very precise, and socially acceptable for monitoring to work

- (0.30 points) There is a possibility for abuse if the car collects too much information

- (0.30 points) Sometimes it's better business to simply repair something in a voided warranty than to lose future business from a good customer

- (0.30 points) Information on monitoring is buried in a contract that most people cannot be expected to read

- (0.30 points) There are other ways (e.g., sight) to determining if a warranty has been voided

- (4.17 points) There are alternative solutions to make this more acceptable

- (1.39 points) If the car only recorded a buffer of information to be used in crash investigations, this would be more acceptable

- (1.39 points) Government regulation should protect the customer from companies having too much power to force concessions and hide monitoring in legalese

- (1.39 points) Customers should be able to get some useful information (e.g., history/use information when reselling a car) out of the monitored data

A.4 NEW TECHNOLOGIES FOR LAW ENFORCEMENT (DAY 4)

A number of advances in information technology, such as thermal imaging devices, surveillance cameras, and face-recognition software, and systems that can pinpoint an individual's position provide exciting new data-gathering capabilities. However, they also lead to a diminishing of individual privacy and add to the question of to what extent technology should be used to capture information about individuals' private lives—where they are, who they are, and what they are doing behind closed doors.

Read the following two scenarios and then discuss the seven questions that follow (three questions on the first scenario and four on the second). Spend about the same amount of time on each of the questions.

A.4.1 Scenario 1

Police can use thermal imaging devices from outside a house to detect patterns of heat being generated from inside. Use of this technology led to the conviction of an Oregon man for growing marijuana in his home. Police used a thermal imager to detect the distinctive heat pattern made by the high-intensity lights that are often used for marijuana cultivation. The police then used this information as the basis for obtaining a search warrant to uncover the contraband. Subsequently, however, the Supreme Court overturned the conviction, finding that the original search warrant should not have been granted, since the thermal image evidence itself constituted an unwarranted search and thus violated the Fourth Amendment.

1. (25 points) One reason that the majority of the court gave for considering the use of thermal imaging an unwarranted search is that citizens have a reasonable expectation of privacy in their own homes. If you do something illegal and are viewed through an open win-

dow, you are not protected by being in your home, because you do not have a reasonable expectation of privacy when it comes to the transparency of glass. But thermal imaging makes one's roof and walls transparent to infra-red radiation. What is the difference between looking through a window in the visual spectrum and looking through a roof in the infra-red? Do you think that thermal imaging is an unwarranted search?

Perspective	Evidence
• (4.17 points) Thermal imaging is an unwarranted search	• (0.60 points) People have a right to expect privacy in their homes
	• (0.60 points) Allowing thermal imaging allows the government nearly unfettered access to monitoring its population
	• (0.60 points) Thermal imaging uses technology to circumvent commonly understood physical barriers protecting privacy (e.g., walls and window shades)
	• (0.60 points) Thermal imaging requires special technology that is not available to or understood by the general population
	• (0.60 points) There is a slippery slope when allowing invasions of privacy

- (0.60 points) Thermal imaging is similar to invading someone's home, which requires a warrant

- (0.60 points) There is nothing stopping police from obtaining a warrant for thermal imaging

• (4.17 points) Thermal imaging is not a problem	• (4.17 points) Since you never know that you've been searched, thermal imagining is not disturbing or invasive
• (4.17 points) Legal and ethical considerations are independent	• (4.17 points) Just because something is legal in the US does not mean that it's legal elsewhere

2. (15 points) If the Oregon man had been growing marijuana plants in his backyard, behind a fence high enough for this practice to be invisible except from the air, and had the evidence the police gathered been aerial photographs, his conviction would have stood. We are used to planes and helicopters flying overhead. As a consequence, we no longer have a reasonable expectation of privacy in our backyards. Do you think that the public has a reasonable expectation of privacy with respect to thermal imaging technology? As it becomes more familiar—as aircraft once did—will this technology no longer constitute an unwarranted search?

Perspective	Evidence
• (1.88 points) Aerial surveillance is not problematic	• (0.47 points) Airplanes do not circumvent physical barriers protecting privacy, but rather simply give a new angle on publicly viewable behavior
	• (0.47 points) With airplanes, you can see the device that is monitoring you
	• (0.47 points) Aircraft are familiar and accessible to the general population
	• (0.47 points) Reason-able people automatically assume no privacy when outside
• (1.88 points) Aerial surveillance should be considered an unwarranted search	• (0.63 points) With airplane surveillance, it's impossible to know when and whether we have been targeted
	• (0.63 points) No one expects a neighbor to take photographs over the fence
	• (0.63 points) People have a right to expect privacy in their back yard, especially if it's fenced
• (3.75 points) There is a difference between random observation and targeted surveillance	None given

- (1.88 points) Privacy can be reasonably violated in cases of emergency

- (0.94 points) If time were not a factor, it would be easy to get a warrant in cases of an emergency

- (0.94 points) In an emergency, the obligation to provide aid overrides the rights to privacy

3. (10 points) Is your answer to the first of these questions affected by your attitude toward the illegality of marijuana? If you think that marijuana should be decriminalized or that possession/cultivation should not be a major felony, suppose instead that the heat signatures had been used as evidence of another crime that you are unambivalent about. How serious would the crime have to be before you changed your mind, if at all?

Perspective	Evidence
• (5.00 points) Severity of the crime is irrelevant	• (2.50 points) Even severe crimes are somewhat protected when done in private
	• (2.50 points) Privacy is a fundamental right that exists independently of the legality of a given activity

A.4.2 Scenario 2

The police department of Tampa, Florida, placed 36 cameras in the popular Ybor City downtown district and connected them to a powerful computer loaded with face-recognition software. Now, everyone who visits the district is subject to having their faces digitally scanned and their noses, cheeks, and chins checked against a mug-shot database of murderers, drug dealers, and other criminals. Tampa officials used a similar system in January, 2001, to scan the crowds of the Superbowl for possible terrorists.

4. (15 points) Law enforcement officials claim that use of the system does not violate any privacy rights and that its use is no different from having more police officers walk around trying to identify suspects from mug shots. Do you agree?

Perspective	Evidence
• (1.88 points) Using cameras in public locations is perfectly acceptable	• (0.31 points) Personally, I wouldn't care
	• (0.31 points) You have no reasonable expectation of privacy while in public
	• (0.31 points) You do not have to go to locations that are monitored
	• (0.31 points) Cameras just make the natural process of recognizing people more efficient
	• (0.31 points) When you're in public, the police have a right to stop you and check you identity against criminal databases

- (1.88 points) Using cameras in public locations is problematic

- (1.88 points) There is a qualitative difference between government and corporate surveillance

---

- (0.31 points) The government has a right and duty to protect public property and ensure public safety

- (0.23 points) In a public place, it's impossible to opt out of surveillance

- (0.23 points) This could lead to the tracking of individuals, which is not acceptable

- (0.23 points) This can lead to abuse and misuse

- (0.23 points) The technology is simply not good enough to work well yet

- (0.23 points) False positives will create a lot of hassle for innocent people

- (0.23 points) The next step after identifying a suspected terrorist is unclear

- (0.23 points) Cameras capture lots of unnecessary, but highly personal information

- (0.23 points) Cameras degrade social trust

- (0.94 points) Citizens have greater freedom to choose whether or not to visit corporate locations

	than they do for public locations
	• (0.94 points) Citizens have constitutional protections against government surveillance that do not apply to corporate surveillance
• (1.88 points) Making decisions based on reasonable expectations is problematic	• (1.88 points) Expectations may vary from person to person

5. (10 points) They also claim that people should expect their privacy is diminished when they visit the crowded public streets of Ybor City, which are filled with restaurants, nightclubs, stores, and thousands of people. Signs in the streets warn visitors that "Smart CCTV is in use." Do you agree that the fact that your privacy is diminished when you are in a crowd justifies this kind of police surveillance?

Perspective	Evidence
• (1.67 points) The crowd is irrelevant to the ethical considerations	• (0.83 points) The software tracks individuals, so the size of the crowd is irrelevant
	• (0.83 points) There is no privacy while out in public to begin with, so the size of the crowd doesn't matter

- (1.67 points) There is
  no privacy in a crowd

- (1.67 points) In a crowd,
  you should expect that
  there is a chance of being
  recognized

- (1.67 points) Crowds
  do not diminish the level
  of privacy

- (0.83 points) Crowds
  increase the level of
  anonymity, which should
  increase privacy

- (0.83 points) You always
  have a certain baseline of
  privacy, that can be height-
  ened (e.g., at home), but
  never removed

---

6. (10 points) Privacy advocates have objected that the
   use of such systems amounts to putting the public in a
   digital police lineup. Is this analogy reasonable?

Perspective	Evidence
- (1.67 points) The digital line-up is a good analogy	- (0.83 points) If people haven't done anything wrong, they have nothing to worry about
	- (0.83 points) Unlike a real line-up, this technology does not waste individuals' time
- (1.67 points) There are better analogies that could be used	- (0.83 points) Looking through mug shots is a more accurate analogy
	- (0.83 points) Putting up wanted posters is a more accurate analogy

- (1.67 points) Comparing cameras to a digital line-up is not correct

- (0.56 points) A line-up is associated with a specific crime

- (0.56 points) In a line-up, the police have already caught the suspected criminal

- (0.56 points) A line-up involves the voluntary participation of non-suspects

7. (15 points) The Superbowl experiment identified nineteen terrorist suspects. If this experiment had been a live law-enforcement use of the system and the suspects had been arrested and successfully prosecuted, would this justify the use of the system? What if the suspects were not successfully prosecuted? What if they were not suspected terrorists but suspected mobsters?

Perspective	Evidence
• (1.50 points) Successful prosecution of the crime is irrelevant	• (1.50 points) Justifying the use of cameras based on the results of their use is circular logic
• (3.00 points) Successful prosecution of the crime justifies the system	None given
• (1.50 points) The level of the crime (e.g., terrorism) is irrelevant	• (0.50 points) Terrorism is often used incorrectly to justify invasions of privacy

	• (0.50 points) There is a slippery slope toward total surveillance if it is allowed in some cases
	• (0.50 points) If there are no problems with the system to begin with, then the level of the crime is irrelevant
• (1.50 points) The level of the crime (e.g., terrorism) matters	• (1.50 points) There is a difference between major crimes (e.g., murder, terrorism) and minor ones (e.g., outstanding parking tickets)
• (3.00 points) It is unclear how to go about measuring the success of a system like this	None given

APPENDIX B

DISCUSSION TRANSCRIPTS

In Chapter 4, I provided a qualitative description of two group discussions. In doing so, I argued that there is reason to believe that the grading metric presented in that section accurately reflected the quality of any given discussion. Below, I present the full transcript of the two discussions.

B.1 A "GOOD" DISCUSSION

(Group 6, Day 1, Online)

```
4/12/2005 4:23:55 PM : Amir has joined the channel
4/12/2005 4:28:42 PM : Scott has joined the channel
4/12/2005 4:29:21 PM : Craig has joined the channel
```

1. **Amir:** hey
2. **Scott:** hi
3. **Amir:** anyone know if this is moderated in any form? or do we just do what we want?
4. **Craig:** I'm not really sure
5. **Craig:** think we will end up with anyone else in the group or is this it?
6. **Scott:** i don't think its directly moderated, but the prof has access to the logs

7. **Scott:** lets wait a minute or two, usually the groups are four people
8. **Amir:** ya
9. **Craig:** alright
10. **Scott:** yeah, lets go with it
11. **Amir:** sure...works for me
12. **Amir:** have you guys read the story?
13. **Scott:** yep, I've read it
14. **Craig:** yup
15. **Amir:** i think blogs and online journals are pretty much public
16. **Amir:** so if you post to them then you should expect them to be read by anyone and everyone
17. **Craig:** yeah, anything on the internet can be read by anyone, so you shouldn't expect them to be private
18. **Scott:** i agree, its on the internet
19. **Craig:** plus, how would anyone know if they were supposed to access it or not?
20. **Scott:** the only way you could possibly expect it to be private is if you had some sort of authentication system
21. **Amir:** true
22. **Craig:** how about number 2?
23. **Amir:** i think that she is being snoopy
24. **Amir:** her best bet is probably to not mention anything about what she read
25. **Craig:** I could see why you might feel guilty about reading a childs journal, online or not
26. **Scott:** she's being snoopy, but its within reason, although i think its different than a physical journal
27. **Amir:** i think it's slightly different

28. **Amir:** you can "hide" physical journals
29. **Craig:** I agree, with reading a physical jour-nal it's considerably more intrusive
30. **Amir:** so i think those might be considered to be more private
31. **Scott:** yeah, and most people have a differ-ent view of privacy in the physical world as opposed to on the internet
32. **Amir:** do you think she should confront alice about it?
33. **Craig:** it depends on how strongly she is opposed to skydiving
34. **Craig:** if she is really adamant that it's not safe, then certainly
35. **Scott:** at this point, both people are adults, in my opinion, so i think have a discussion about it is not something that would be harm-ful
36. **Amir:** i guess it depends on whether or not the mother is supporting her daughter
37. **Craig:** I see acting on it as really more a matter on how much she feels she should involve herself in her childrens' buisness
38. **Craig:** and less on the importance of the source
39. **Amir:** ya i agree with that as well
40. **Craig:** alright, so how about number 3
41. **Craig:**?
42. **Amir:** what about the issue of carol reading her kids' journals again?
43. **Craig:** oh
44. **Scott:** you mean the blogs?
45. **Amir:** ya
46. **Craig:** again, I would say that she can continue if she wants because it's freely available,

but if her children ask her not to she should
stop

47. **Amir:** perhaps she should improve her relationship with her kids rather than snoop around
and read their blogs without telling them

48. **Scott:** i think its up to her whether or not she
should read them, and if the children don't
want them read, take them down or restart the
blog under a truly anonymous name

49. **Craig:** agreed

50. **Amir:** that's only possible if the kids find
out that carol has been reading their blogs

51. **Amir:** but it makes sense

52. **Amir:** alright, #3?

53. **Craig:** I don't have a blog, but occasionally
I'll put a quote or something in an AIM away
message and it's really irritating to get
nagged about that. I certainly don't see it
as invasive, but it's just kind of an annoy-
ance

54. **Scott:** no, i really can't relate to it, i
don't have any sort of online blog, or even
a physical diary

55. **Amir:** i can kinda relate on a personal
level...i went skydiving and i just didn't
bother to tell my parents because i didn't
really know how they would react about it

56. **Amir:** i don't keep a journal either so nothing
about that

57. **Scott:** i make sure to think about what i put
online, cause i know anyone could find out

58. **Amir:** but putting myself in their shoes, i
think i would be pretty annoyed

59. **Amir:** one of my cousins used my AIM account
once and it ticked me off

60. **Craig:** so we agree it's annoying but not fundamentally offencive?
61. **Amir:** i think there are plenty of things that go on within my circle of friends that i wouldn't want to discuss with my parents
62. **Scott:** yeah, me too, thats why i generally don't post anything like that
63. **Amir:** ya annoying but not fundamentally offencive
64. **Craig:** well certainly, but you wouldn't post them online, would you?
65. **Amir:** nope i don't think i would post online
66. **Craig:** okay, so number 4?
67. **Amir:** yop
68. **Amir:** i guess it matters a little bit as to what alice is planning to do
69. **Amir:** if she were suicidal it would be a much bigger deal than if she wanted to get a tattoo
70. **Craig:** since I didn't have any objections to carol using the information she found, I still object even less to using it in a more serious circumstance
71. **Amir:** same
72. **Craig:** I again think it's back to a matter of balancing respect for your children and trying to protect them
73. **Scott:** if it was something very serious, then i think it would be carols, and even anyone's responsiblity to tell someone that could help her
74. **Amir:** however, wild orgies must be permiited
75. **Scott:** haha
76. **Craig:** absolutely

77. **Amir:** so we have a concensus that we would object even less if there was a serious situation?
78. **Craig:** yeah, I think so
79. **Scott:** yep
80. **Craig:** alright, 5 then: does the age matter?
81. **Craig:** I again say not really
82. **Amir:** ya i think the principle is the same regardless of the age
83. **Craig:** so, on to 6?
84. **Amir:** in reality though, i think most parents would let their kids start making their decisions by the time they are in their twenties
85. **Craig:** you would think
86. **Scott:** yeah, age shouldn't be an issue
87. **Amir:** i think #6 is less of an issue if the blogs were somehow tied to the company
88. **Scott:** regarding number 6, i think its the same matter of whether or not its public
89. **Amir:** if they are public blogs then i think that we are on the same page is with the earlier situation
90. **Craig:** If carol is an employeer I see it as a different issue, I don't think that carol can act on the information
91. **Scott:** you can still circulate resumes when you are working, and even get other job offers, you just keep it quiet
92. **Amir:** ya
93. **Craig:** I know it's kind of hypcritical, but it seems like if an employer is using information that you post to fire you it is an invasion of your free speach

94. **Craig:** whereas a parent may be using it to repremand you, it's not in so much of a formal situation: they don't really have control over you

95. **Amir:** ya but i think the same thing would happen if an employee were to directly face their employer with such an issue

96. **Scott:** but then thats saying an employer can't fire you for something you said at work?

97. **Amir:** i'm not sure about how free speech rights are carried out in this situation

98. **Craig:** saying something at work is different from saying it on a street corner

99. **Scott:** how?

100. **Amir:** i agree with Craig on this one

101. **Amir:** i think that the work environment is different

102. **Craig:** if you go up to your boss and call him an idiot while at work you are being provokative

103. **Amir:** some things that are acceptable outside of a work place are not acceptable at work

104. **Scott:** so are you saying that if you call your boss an idiot, at work, he should have the right to fire you or whatever, but not if you say it on the street corner, and he happens to be standing right behind you?

105. **Craig:** I do think there is a fundamental difference

106. **Amir:** true

107. **Amir:** in reality the two might be the same

108. **Amir:** but there is a fundamental difference

109. **Craig:** now whether or not your calling him an idiot on the street corner is slanderous and

could get you sued is another matter, but I
don't think it's comething you should be able
to be fired for
110. **Scott:** so then what if you divulge company
secrets on a street corner?
111. **Amir:** i'm not surprised that people get fired
for this kind of stuff. i'm sure the employer
comes up with issues such as employees being
ineffecient because of their dissatisfaction
and they use that reason to let their employees go
112. **Craig:** I mean, extending that idea you could
be prevented from voicing political opinions
because you risk your employeer firing you,
your employeer can't do that

4/12/2005 5:00:56 PM : Warren has joined the channel

113. **Amir:** well calling your boss an idiot might
not break company rules
114. **Amir:** but revealing secrets probably breaks
some rules
115. **Craig:** well divulging secrects probably breaks
a non-disclosure contract
116. **Amir:** ya
117. **Scott:**
118. **Craig:** depends on who your employer is
119. **Craig:** true

4/12/2005 5:01:40 PM : Warren has left the channel
4/12/2005 5:01:50 PM : Warren has joined the channel

120. **Scott:** you can be released from the military
by making politcal comments in uniform
121. **Craig:** but again, that's on the job, not in a
public forum

122. **Amir:** well, do we think it's fair or unfair?

123. **Scott:** we digress

124. **Craig:** I think it would be unfair to be fired for something you posted on a personal blog

125. **Scott:** i personally think its fair, the information is just as public as in the first case

126. **Amir:** I'm pretty borderline on this one

127. **Amir:** i agree that the information is just as public

128. **Craig:** I think it **would** be fair to be fired for something you posted on a company blog or even a personal blog in which you use your position with the company extensivly (i.e., to give you credibility or some such)

129. **Amir:** but then again if you aren't breaking company rules by voicing your opinion then you shouldn't be fired

130. **Warren:** Not sure how I'm this late for an online class, but I'll jump in here I guess.

131. **Amir:** sure

132. **Amir:** we're on #6

133. **Amir:** discussing if it's fair to fire the employee

134. **Scott:** good job Warren :-)

135. **Amir:** i think it's completely fair if the blog is a company blog or somehow related to the company

136. **Scott:** that also raises the issue of whether or not the rules of where you post the blog states that you give them rights to all the posts

137. **Amir:** and it's also fair to fire the employee if the personal unhappiness is causing loss in efficieny
138. **Warren:** Were the blog a company blog, yes, but it seems that it's a personal one, so you should be fine.
139. **Scott:** the case i know of where this has happened in the past was a microsoft employee got fired for posting a picture he took at work of microsoft recieving a shipment of apple g%s
140. **Scott:** g5s*
141. **Amir:** lol
142. **Scott:** which probably broke some sort of rule on taking pictures
143. **Amir:** ya
144. **Amir:** i think this situation depends too much on company polices
145. **Amir:** policies*
146. **Amir:** and without this info it's pretty hard to make a solid judgement on what fair and what's not
147. **Warren:** I think that it has to do with the position that the person has at the company, too. If they're a public figure, then it affects their job and daily interactions differently if everyone knows they're unhappy.
148. **Craig:** I know a guy who was a TA at tech that got fired for posting something inflame about how much some (unrelated to his TAing class) professor sucked
149. **Warren:** For example, public university, if it were a professor, they'd be gone on the spot. public blog or not.

150. **Amir:** ya
151. **Amir:** so do we agree that it depends too much on the situation?
152. **Craig:** I think so
153. **Warren:** Yep, as TA's, we represent the school to other students, and as such, lose rights to drudge around in the muck on flame
154. **Warren:** Yep
155. **Amir:**
156. **Scott:** are you still holding to the employee being fired regardless of the situation?
157. **Scott:** hold on a sec
158. **Scott:** sorry about that, just got a call about a scholarship
159. **Amir:** nice
160. **Scott:** but yea, i think its fair to be able to be fired for posting something to a blog, but not necessarily reasonable
161. **Amir:** works for me
162. **Amir:** it takes too long to discuss stuff online
163. **Amir:** i wonder what the researcher thinks of this
164. **Craig:** I think it's a bad idea, but it worked out better than I expected
165. **Scott:** yeah, i thought it was going to be a massive chat with everyone
166. **Amir:** that would suck
167. **Scott:** it gets people talking more than in class i would imagine
168. **Scott:** yeah, it would have
169. **Warren:** I think that online discussions could be great, but trying to shove them into a set block of time is a mistake

170. **Amir:** ya i think people might be less reluctant to talk online
171. **Warren:** The asynchrony of the conversation is partially what makes it awesome
172. **Warren:** Not that that's even a word.
173. **Amir:** lol
174. **Craig:** what would you rather? like a newsgroup style discussion?
175. **Amir:** i dunno
176. **Craig:** (with regards to a set block of time)
177. **Warren:** Well, I think it could be a persistent chatroom with ongoing issues, somewhat like a newsgroup but without the overhead
178. **Warren:** designed to take chat-style messages
179. **Amir:** i prefer the chatroom type interaction over a newsgroup
180. **Craig:** sooo... a BBS kind of thing?
181. **Warren:** Depending on how people were using it, it would conform to the use. If people were sending lots of messages, call it a chatroom, that's how it acts
182. **Warren:** but if only one person is there, and drops a message or a few, the history is saved and people see it when they next enter
183. **Craig:** The problem I would see with that is the slow response time...
184. **Amir:** Warren, could you see our earlier discussion?
185. **Warren:** Nope
186. **Craig:** and with a slow response time you become less personally invested in the conversation
187. **Amir:** that sucks

188. **Scott:** although it would be nice that way you could just login, drop something down in the middle of the night, and its up later for the next day
189. **Amir:** ya
190. **Craig:** if it were this style but with a history already up when you logged in, I could see that as viable
191. **Amir:** i guess we can log off now?
192. **Warren:** Well, it's like a conversation, just stretched out indefinitely. I think that attempting to pack it into a 1 hour class is just a mismatch of the technology to application
193. **Craig:** possibly but, for example, in english 2 we were required to post to WebX
194. **Scott:** yeah
195. **Craig:** and that really never became a conversation of any sort
196. **Warren:** Yeah, the webx stuff was rotten when I did it too
197. **Amir:** i never used it but i heard it sucked
198. **Warren:** obligatory post, and then you never looked at anything else
199. **Amir:** haha
200. **Craig:** exactly
201. **Craig:** anyways, are we done or should we expect that we are going to get some more instruction at some point?
202. **Amir:** i'm gonna go with done
203. **Amir:** are you guys gonna stick around?

4/12/2005 5:19:11 PM : Craig has left the channel

204. **Amir:** i guess not
205. **Warren:** I think I'm going to just sit here with it open

206. **Scott:** i guess we can just vacate
207. **Scott:** i might
208. **Amir:** ya
209. **Amir:** I'm out
210. **Warren:** later
211. **Amir:** see ya

4/12/2005 5:19:33 PM : Amir has left the channel
4/12/2005 5:20:06 PM : Craig has joined the channel

212. **Craig:** I'm thinking no
213. **Warren:** I'm just going to leave it open, on account of me being so late to start with. Not that it'll make a difference, but I figure it can't hurt anything.
214. **Craig:** that sounds reasonable
215. **Craig:** but if we're done, I think I'm just going to go walk my dog
216. **Craig:** see you all thusday

4/12/2005 5:22:22 PM : Craig has left the channel
4/12/2005 5:34:09 PM : Warren has left the channel
4/12/2005 5:38:20 PM : Scott has left the channel

B.2 A "Poor" Discussion

(Group 3, Day 1, Face-to-Face)

Note: For Jay, I often observed the others leaning in when he spoke. Presumably, since I couldn't hear him that well either, he did not speak very loudly.

1. **David:** Alright. So, have y'all read yet? Are you still reading?
2. **Jay:** I read it.
3. **David:** Alright. Have you finished?
4. **Brian:** I've read the scenario questions.

5. **David:** Alright, well. I don't really think that you should think anything on your blog is private.
6. **Brian:** Yeah, true.
7. **David:** I mean, I think if you're savvy enough to have a blog, you know what Google is. You know you can find anything anywhere, within reason. So, if they didn't want...
8. **Jay:** I think publishing information and then expecting it to be private is very stupid.
9. **David:** Yeah.
10. **Gavin:** Well, it's... (interrupted)
11. **Brian:** If you don't put something password protected or whatever on the Internet, it's wide open. And, even sometimes when it's password protected, it's still accessible.
12. **Gavin:** Well... (interrupted)
13. **Jay:** It goes beyond just stuff that isn't encrypted or doesn't have some kind of security measures in place. This is something that's usually, like, actively published on some kind of site.
14. **Gavin:** Well, the thing is... With this, it's security through anonymity. Usually, you don't know who the person is in particular. But, since they're using almost like a weak form of encryption, with their anonymity being so weak that they can figure it out, that, you know, it is pretty much public. But it's... There's almost a sense of known anonymity with it. That's really what they're getting to.
15. **Brian:** I mean, then again, you say that, but if I use the same... If I use my gte name, gte account number, as

my blog screen name, you shouldn't expect someone not to figure it out.

16. **Gavin:** But it's also the same thing as if I used a weak form of encryption that's been cracked and I've known that, you know, I shouldn't go around thinking that, "Hey! I'm behind this wall."

17. **Brian:** Right. Exactly.

(long pause)

18. **Jay:** Usually, usually they're going to <unintelligible> screen names of people looking for something like that. Like you said earlier, they use the same handles that they use for everything else. They're really not trying to be anonymous. They're just trying to come up with a screen name that's not taken.

19. **Brian:** To some extent, they are anon... (interrupted)

20. **Jay:** I can't go to a blog site and register my name as Bob. I'm sure someone's got that already, so I've got to come up with something else. It's not cause I'm trying to be sneaky or trying to come up with a secret identity or anything, it's just that I'm trying to come up with a log in name.

21. **Brian:** Well, to some extent, you are being anonymous in that a complete random stranger wouldn't have a clue where to start.

(Ed walks up)

22. **Gavin:** That's such a good point

23. **Brian:** But some of the <unintelligible> figure it out.

24. **Ed (Instructor):** So, what do you think, guys?

25. **Jay:** I'm <unintelligible> what I can say about group blogs. <unintelligible> go around saying that people who blog things are students.
26. **Gavin:** Especially since it's being recorded. (all laugh)
27. **Ed (Instructor):** I know. It is strange, isn't it? People reveal all kinds of things weird things that they probably wouldn't in their webpages necessarily. Although, a few years ago, people did that as well.
28. **Gavin:** The argument that I've been making is that they have a sense of anonymity and... (interrupted)
29. **Ed (Instructor):** Yeah, exactly.
30. **Gavin:** ... and it's almost like encryption. So, she picked a weak identifier, essentially. She's picking a weak encryption, so it's weak anonymity, almost.
31. **Ed (Instructor):** Right.
32. **Brian:** I would say it goes more than that. This is also a psychological effect because there's no direct consequences immediately after... Like, if I tell you straight up that I cheated on the last test, I'll instantaneously feel the results. But, if I put it on a blog, then I can be kind of daring, showing off to all of my friends, and the risk is kind of ok that you may or may not find out about it, because... It feels like all of my friends get to see how cool and bad I am, while I can kind of skirt the consequences.
33. **Ed (Instructor):** Yeah, it's... So, that's actually a comment about motivation, the motivation that people might post things... Essentially, they take risks by posting things that they might not say face-to-face.

34. **Brian:** Say the things that they want to say, but they're too afraid to say in reality, because if you give me a disapproving look, instantly, I know that I did something wrong. On the Internet, I <unintelligible>
35. **Gavin:** Well, that's also like the rumor mill that's going behind someone's back and talking about it. They're still at risk that it might get back to the person.
36. **Brian:** But, you're not going to think about that. If you're talking to someone, you're like, "Oh, she blabs everything to everyone. I'm not going to say anything to here." But, you're online, you're like, "Eh…" Certain things, you just don't think <unintelligible>.
37. **David:** It's definitely (not?) the same thing as going through someone's journal. Like we said earlier, you're definitely publishing it online, making the document available on a server. Whereas, when you put it in a journal, that's understood to be your personal space.
38. **Brian:** And it's kept in a secure location.
39. **Ed (Instructor):**I get… Do you think that everybody sees it that way? Because, sometimes people react to technology… They use analogies and metaphors, even through it's technically available. It's not highly encrypted. Nevertheless, if it's something which is a fairly closed community?the URL isn't advertised?it's a little bit like putting something in a journal and not keeping it in a safe deposit box, but just hiding it under your bed or not leaving it lying around. There's still a possibility that people will find out.

40. **Brian:** With a journal, there's an expectation of privacy in that it says journal on the front of it. We all know that in American culture that's usually a private item, whereas if you put something on the Internet and you don't have it password protected or SSL or something, then why can't I go and read it. You shouldn't post it on the Internet.

41. **David:** To have a more accurate analogy, you wouldn't be putting something on the Internet. You'd put it on your personal computer, if you wanted a journal. If the purpose is for your personal records, then there's no reason to put it available online.

42. **Ed (Instructor):** There's still the communication with friends or the outside world. You just don't want some people to read it. … Actually, <unintelligible> thinking about the psychology from Alice's point of view, think about Carol's as well here. Question number two is kind of interesting about… Particularly the fact that she's a parent as well. This isn't just an abstract case of somebody reading something by somebody else that they don't really know. I mean, there's a deeply contextual thing here that there's a relationship that's been going on for a couple of decades. We shouldn't abstract away from the situation too much, maybe. Think about what <unintelligible> she's doing and whether what she's doing is right. Whether Alice has a reasonable expectation of privacy or not, do you think that parents should do this sort of thing? Under what conditions is it reasonable or whatever?

43. **David:** So, it seems kind of related to number four, where if it's a concerned parent and they're finding out information about their children, it might be a little more harmful than skydiving. I mean, skydiving is a risky activity, but joining a cult might be considered slightly more dangerous. I don't know.

(Ed walks up)

44. **Brian:** My feeling is still the same. If you post something on the Internet, you should expect everyone in the world to read it, including your parents. I mean, everyone is curious. I've looked at my parents names to see what comes up, <unintelligible> to find or something.

45. **Gavin:** What's that? Eagle searching or something?

46. **Brian:** What?

47. **Gavin:** Where you stick your own name in and Google it.

(long pause)

48. **Gavin:** Yeah, I don't view it as snooping at all. I mean, it's on the Internet. It's not like she's going through her emails and stuff like that that have been stolen off her computer. It's not like she's listening on the phone or anything like that. It's out there in public…

49. **Brian:** If it was a mailing list and not a blog, and somehow she tapped her way into the mailing list, not <unintelligible>

50. **Gavin:** Yeah, yeah.

51. **David:** Again, with email lists, there's that password protection that's an obvious form of keeping it within a certain circle.

52. **Brian:** And it's... (interrupted)

53. **David:** Putting it on the Internet without any restrictions whatsoever, any disclaimer, it's just... (interrupted)

54. **Gavin:** Or any password or anything like that... I mean, she could have just password protected it, give the username and password to her friends. They can read it, post on it... (interrupted)

55. **Brian:** And, even if you have a username and password set up and even if it isn't very secure, it, at least, sets forth that you have an expectation that only certain people read it, whereas in this situation, you can find it in a search engine, you can <unintelligible>

56. **Jay:** Digging through someone's <unintelligible>... We said that already. It's like if you took a sign and wrote, "Gone to a drunken orgy. Be back later." And taped it to your door.

57. **Gavin:** Yeah, exactly.

58. **Jay:** If your Mom finds that and gets mad, "That was in my room!"

59. **Brian:** There's kids that are like... In my Freshman year, kids would put stuff like that on their dorm room doors. You know, it's like, "I'm so cool. I'm going to this drunken orgy. Be back later." Yeah, if their Mom or someone walked in and sees it, they can't be upset about that. It's the same thing.

60. **David:** I don't put stuff in my away message because my parents have AIM.

61. **Brian:** Yeah, exactly. I don't put stuff in my away message because I don't want people knowing where I am. If I'm not there, it's because I don't want you knowing if I'm there or not.

62. **Jay:** I would have to take personal responsibility my parents, introducing them to… helping them get on the Internet. It's actually my uncle who talked my Mom into getting on MSN Messenger, but I helped. I see her online, and it's just like, "Dang it!"

63. **Gavin:** Block, block, block.

64. **Jay:** The thing with MSN Messenger is that there is no away message. It's just an away status.

65. **Gavin:** The funny thing is that my parents don't hop on the Internet to, you know, do instant messaging or anything, but my Dad plays Red Alert, Command and Conquer: Red Alert. It's hilarious.

66. **David:** Alright, question three. How would you feel if you were in Alice or Bob's situation? I would expect anyone to find my information that I published. That's how I'd feel.

67. **Jay:** I understand from the stuff that my girlfriend puts in her blog that she wouldn't tell her parents directly. I've told her, "Why are you doing this?"

68. **Gavin:** Yeah.

69. **Brian:** It's funny to me how people always have the need to want to tell their secrets even through they know that it's not going to work for the best <unintelligible>.

(long pause)

70. **Jay:** Another thing is more and more people on blogs are in a blog ring. So, if you can find one person that you know, you can find all of their friends. They usually post comments on everybody else's stuff so you can figure out who's who quickly.

71. **Gavin:** What about number six?

72. **David:** Other than the obvious remark that firing someone because they're considering a job offer... If that's not in the company policy, then they shouldn't be able to do that. But, if you state... When you join the company, you're informed that if you are considering taking a job at somewhere else, you should terminate your employment here. Then, you shouldn't expect that just because you don't tell your employer that he doesn't know.

73. **Jay:** If you're considering a job offer from the competition, then you'd better quit anyway. So, <unintelligible> firing <unintelligible> what's happening to you.

74. **Gavin:** What about a worker who's, you know, something a little bit better... Interoffice rivalries, writing about that. Or, maybe, how your recent project hasn't gone very well, and maybe not everyone knows about that. What about that?

75. **Brian:** I'd still feel the same way. If anyone can read it, you shouldn't be posting stuff on there you don't want everyone to read.

76. **Gavin:** Do you think it's reasonable that they got fired though for that?

77. **Brian:** I mean, if you're a boss and someone is admitting that they're a slacker on the job or telling how

much they hate you, I'd fire them. I'm not going to spend all day searching on employees names trying to find out, but it came to my attention one way or another, it just makes sense. As a company, you have to make decisions that affect the bottom line. If someone's being a problem...

78. **Gavin:** Also, in private companies, pay rates aren't known. So, if someone were to post pay rates of a certain number of people, maybe not even including themselves, do you think they should be held responsible for that?

79. **Brian:** If they post someone else's pay rate?

80. **Gavin:** Yeah.

81. **David:** And that was private information...? (interrupted)

82. **Brian:** Yeah, I would say that would be an invasion of privacy, if something like that happened.

(long pause)

83. **Gavin:** Anything else on this topic?

84. **David:** So, I guess number five is more aimed at the other side of the argument. So, we were making the argument that... (interrupted)

85. **Gavin:** The other way. Yeah.

86. **David:** ...wasn't ok for them to be snooping, then would it be ok if they were a minor? Not a minor, but younger versus older, I guess. No?

(long pause)

87. **Jay:** If they were talking about getting drunk underage, it would make a difference.

88. **David:** That's true.

(long pause)

89. **Brian:** Having a sex change operation? That's such a common thing that parents worry about for their kids. (laughs)
90. **David:** "I knew it!"
91. **Gavin:** "That's alright, Billy. When you were young, we all thought that you were a girl anyways."
92. **Brian:** What if kids read the parents' blogs talking about how much they hated their kids or something?
93. **Jay:** That'd be pretty bad.
94. **David:** Yeah, I think that would raise some foster home issues. Unfit parenthood.
95. **Gavin:** Negligence.
96. **Brian:** The government comes in and takes your kids away.
97. **David:** Have y'all heard of the...? (interrupted)
98. **Gavin:** What if that... the Health Services went around reading parents' blogs about their kids?
99. **David:** Yeah.
100. **Gavin:** What about that?
101. **Brian:** House Services?
102. **Gavin:** Like, Health Services.
103. **Brian:** Oh, Health Services.
104. **Gavin:** Health Services.
105. **David:** Take away your kids if you... (interrupted)
106. **Brian:** <unintelligible>
107. **Gavin:** Yeah.
108. **David:** I don't know about that.
109. **Gavin:** Is that crossing the boundary of the government's...? (interrupted)

110. **David:** I mean… (interrupted)
111. **Gavin:** Snooping.
112. **David:** I guess a similar situation would be insurance companies using the Internet to search for any kind of information that would…
113. **Brian:** That you listed?
114. **David:** Yeah.
115. **Gavin:** That you listed. Like, "I'm a smoker" or something like… Maybe back then when I filled out the form, I wasn't a smoker, but now I've taken up smoking.
116. **David:** You failed to inform your insurance company, but they found out anyway.

(long pause)

117. **Jay:** What if they said that they were involve in drunken orgies, but they didn't, and their parents kicked them out of the house for it?
118. **Brian:** That's just being stupid.
119. **Gavin:** (laughs) Yeah, at that point, you might as well go ahead and go to the drunken orgy.
120. **David:** "I'll show you, Mom."
121. **Gavin:** You got punished… (interrupted)
122. **Brian:** That's just like completely poor management of your life if you're trying to piss your parents off like that.
123. **David:** Have y'all ever heard of tarblog?
124. **Gavin:** Of what?
125. **David:** Tarblog. T-A-R-B-L-O-G. It's a blog that was started by a teacher that worked at a special school.

They just recorded stories of their retarded students and whatever happens in the classroom.

126. **Brian:** That's horrible.

127 **David:** Yeah. It's pretty horrible, and the stories are hilarious, but I don't... I never even found out what ever happened to whoever started it or whoever continued it, but that would be an interesting blog to bring up in discussion. I don't know if they got fired or if parents raised complaints and they didn't get fired or they did get fired. Either way, I think they would have to change jobs whether or not they got fired, if parents of their students found out.

128. **Gavin:** Well, I know a lot of that stuff is supposed to be kept quiet. Like, what happens in the special classrooms only stays in there. Teachers aren't supposed to be going around... even if it's disciplinary problems, like, that the kid is a maniac during my classes during the special classes. They're not supposed to go out and tell the other teachers that he's such a problem. So, maybe the teacher crossed that boundary in releasing this to the public.

129. **Jay:** My mom works in special ed. She'll come home and talk about how pissed off she is at some kid.

130. **Gavin:** I mean, that's still within...

131. **Jay:** Anh...

132. **Brian:** I feel like there is definitely, when you're dealing with stuff like that, an expectation that you're not going to go like, "This kid's an idiot." I think it's just a decency for another human being. You're not supposed to treat them with...

133. **Jay:** "Damn, this kid's retarded. No wait!" (interrupted)
134. **Gavin:** "We've already known that."
135. **Jay:** "That's why they're in special ed."
136. **Gavin:** Oh, but like, "He chews on his pens" or something like that. It could be something as small as that or something bigger.
137. **David:** So, what about number three? What would you do if you wanted to publish some things with certain people, but not others?
138. **Gavin:** Password protect it. Public key, private key encryption.
139. **Brian:** An email list, so that I know that only they will get it. I guess some of them might forward it, but I trust my friends.
140. **Jay:** <unintelligible>
141. **Gavin:** Public, private key encryption. Reduce the amount of IPs they can come in from. There's steps you can talk.
142. **Brian:** Be like, "Hey, Joe. I did this, how about you?"
143. **Jay:** Ever think that <unintelligible> to care. Here's the impression she's is a hacker. I don't think there's a whole like that you're going to have to do to keep your Mom from snooping in. Just something other than publicly publishing it... (interrupted)
144. **Brian:** Do most blogs offer password protection? I've never used one.
145. **David:** I think some might have a members-only type of thing. Live Journal, I know, has... (interrupted)

146. **Gavin:** Even something like FaceBook. It restricts who can view it by the <unintelligible>. So, right there, I don't think my parents can get access to it.

147. **David:** Well, I mean, if you publish your profile link, they have available... There's like a link that you can give out to anyone even if they don't subscribe or if they are not a member of the FaceBook, where they can access your profile. But, ...

148. **Brian:** Oh really?

149. **David:** It's like, it's your FaceBook ID number plus some other number. If you go to the site that is your profile once you're logged in, it just... The URL has some get-value for your ID number.

150. **Brian:** You can just give that to anybody?

151. **David:** Yeah.

152. **Brian:** So, it's not that secure.

153. **David:** Yeah, but I believe that your profile link is only accessible from your account. So, if you don't ever want to publish that link to anybody, then you just don't give it out.

154. **Brian:** I got you.

(long pause)

155. **Brian:** So, anyway. I guess you just password protect something.

156. **David:** Fair enough.

157. **Jay:** My girlfriend definitely has the link in her AIM profile.

158. **Brian:** Does she talk about you in it?

159. **Jay:** No. Not really.

160. **Brian:** That's probably a good thing. I'd be mad at some girl if she was like, "And, Brian and I did this on Thursday. Blah, blah blah."

(long pause)

161. **David:** What about people who don't know how to password protect websites?
162. **Gavin:** There's a checkbox here. That's a lock.
163. **David:** But, what if there isn't a checkbox?
164. **Brian:** Then don't use it.
165. **Gavin:** They have to know that what they're publishing is public and that there are methods that they can make it private.
166. **Brian:** If they need to have it done bad enough, but they don't know how to do it, then they'll go seek out someone who does. I mean, it won't be that hard for them to find a CS major and get it straightened out. It's just like, if you want something… You're not going to buy an ad in the AJC and post your life story, just because that's the only way to get your friends to find out what's going on in your life.
167. **David:** Alright. That's a good point.
168. **Gavin:** But not tell everyone what page it's on.
169. **Brian:** "I thought you'd never figure it out. I called myself the Kid from Down Under. You're not supposed to know who that was." You can probably even, with something like that, just search for their friends' names and see if you can find out who someone is. If they refer to locations often enough, that sort of

things. You don't even have to know the screen name
or whatever.

170. **David:** Oh yeah.

171. **Brian:** Heuristics.

172. **David:** Google stalking

173. **Gavin:** Have you seen the new Google maps thing?

174. **David:** Yeah.

175. **Gavin:** Someone combined it with the sales and rent-
ing on Craigslist. So, there's points all throughout
Atlanta. They can just click on it and it will show the
pictures of that apartment or that house. Like, how
much the going rate is for it and stuff like that.

176. **Brian:** Really? Where's that?

177. **Gavin:** Search like "Craigslist" and… (interrupted)

178. **Brian:** Craig?

179. **Gavin:** Craig. Like C-R-A-I-G-S list. I think that's
what it is.

180. **Brian:** (Writes it down and shows it the paper to 2:)

181. **Gavin:** Yeah. It's like a… Craigslist is like this big
want ad and, you know, stuff like that. And, they
combined Craigslist with Google ads. It shows the
points all throughout Atlanta where apartments are
and where houses are for sale.

182. **Brian:** Just click on it and you can see…? (interrupted)

183. **Gavin:** Just click on it and you can see the photo of it
and everything.

184. **Brian:** Didn't Lycos or something do a search
where you could search buildings and see pictures of
them?

185. **Gavin:** Amazon did a… They actually took cars. They set up a camera in the window pointing out the passenger's side and drove up and down street.
186. **Brian:** No way!
187. **Gavin:** And, correlating the GPS with the, ah…
188. **Brian:** The video…
189. **Gavin:** The video, they are able to say, "Ok. This is this and this is this." Then, they also did rakings, because sometimes it's off by a little bit because GPS isn't perfect.
190. **Brian:** Especially in big cities.
191. **Gavin:** So, people can say, "Oh. It wasn't there. It was actually this one." Stuff like that.
192. **David:** Have you seen the supposed Area 51 zoom in on Google maps?
193. **Gavin:** Yeah. I've looked at that myself. You can actually, on one of the… (interrupted)
194. **Brian:** Wait, wait, wait. Area 51 is there?
195. **Gavin:** Yeah. It's there.
196. **Brian:** Really?
197. **Gavin:** Yeah. They actually allowed the satellites to go over it. But, I've done… I've done searches for… (interrupted)
198. **Brian:** What about…? (interrupted)
199. **Gavin:** …myself because I know where the B-2 bombers are stationed and stuff like that. I've searched for that. You can actually see a B-2 bomber sitting on the tarmac, just sitting there.
200. **David:** It's like this big… (interrupted)

201. **Brian:** There are places where they don't allow satellites to go over.
202. **Gavin:** No. The government will try to grab the photos back. They'll pay the company not to release them. But, satellites are allowed to go over anywhere. It's due to international treaty and stuff like that.
203. **Brian:** Oh really? Because I know... You know Roland(?), NASA's? I got that and, like, half of Nevada isn't there and stuff.
204. **Gavin:** Mmm. Hmm. It's because NASA's government too.
205. **Brian:** That makes sense. And, uh, what was the other one?
206. **Gavin:** Terra has started... (interrupted)
207. **Brian:** Cuba wasn't there either, which as really retarded.
208. **Gavin:** Terra server was bought out by Microsoft. Now, if you want to print a page, or anything like that, you have to buy it. But, they actually have... They have pretty good resolution. It's basically about the same as the Google one, I think. Who is the other one?
209. **Brian:** Google.
210. **Gavin:** Google. So, it's about the same resolution, and it covers everywhere. I mean, it covered Area 51. That's where they got it from, I'm sure. The B-2 bomber. I looked that one up myself. I'll send you the link if you want.
211. **David:** Alright. I want to see a B-2 bomber.
212. **Gavin:** It's just sitting on the tarmac. Just sitting there. You can tell the shape and everything.

213. **Brian:** They may need to look in Nevada because there's lots of stuff out there.
214. **Gavin:** You can see the pot holes from the nukes and stuff.
215. **Brian:** From what?
216. **Gavin:** The nukes and stuff that they tested.
217. **Brian:** Yeah, yeah, yeah. I was out there for a coop assignment, and driving at night through the desert, you could just see flashes in the distance over the hills. I was like, whatever's going on back there.
218. **Jay:** <unintelligible> grow a third eyeball <unintelligible>.
219. **Brian:** Yeah. I mean, it wasn't that kind. I'm pretty sure if it was a nuke, I would have known. But it would be just like... The sky was kind of bright, and then it would just fade away.
220. **Gavin:** It could be artillery testing or something like that... (interrupted)
221. **Brian:** I'm sure it was something. It wasn't <unintelligible>... (interrupted)
222. **Gavin:** Bombing run or something like that. I'm sure the government has a better secret base now that Area 51 up. And, it has been up for a while, so they've been searching for land for ages.
223. **Brian:** I'm sure they underground stuff, probably.
224. **Gavin:** I mean, they probably have... They do have bases out in the middle of nowhere in the Pacific that they can do stuff like that. That they beat the heck out of back in the 60's.

(long pause)

225. **Jay:** So, blogs...
226. **Brian:** Yeah.
227. **David:** Are there any questions we haven't...
    (interrupted)
228. **Gavin:** We already beat that horse.

(long pause)

229. **Brian:** This is how group discussions really go.
230. **Gavin:** Do we have enough time? I should be able to
    pull up the... I'll see if I can pull it up.
231. **Brian:** Yeah, pull it up.
232. **Gavin:** I used to have it saved in a document, but...
233. **Jay:** Imagine a field that represents CS 4001. "Imag-
    ine a horse that is this class. Imagine us standing there
    beating that dead horse."
234. **Gavin:** I'm going to go taping it (?).
235. **Brian:** I wonder how... I don't know... How seriously
    you can take this research. Because no one is just going
    to sit here and be like this, "Do you want to talk about
    this?" "No." "Alright, me neither." But, I've definitely
    be in group discussions where it's like, "What do you
    guys think?" "They shouldn't expect any privacy."
    "Yeah, I agree." "Alright" "So you see the game on
    Friday? I liked it." I mean, I don't know...
236. **Jay:** I don't know how these online small groups are
    going to go. No one is going to be able to focus on
    <unintelligible>
237. **Brian:** Yeah, for real. There's no way no one's going
    to...

238. **Jay:** "Bob slaps Brian with a wet trout." That's all it's going to be.

239. **Brian:** Especially if we're all anonymous or whatever. Then, you can just be like, "You know, I really don't think I was treated correctly on that last test" in the middle of the discussion.

240. **David:** I'm definitely going to go and get myself l33t translators and before I say anything, just put it through a filter and just copy and paste that. It's going to be great.

241. **Gavin:** I can't believe you couldn't post that on the swiki: the paper <unintelligible> that posted on the Internet and the translation.

242. **David:** Have you seen the Microsoft guide to l33t speak?

243. **Gavin:** Parent's guide to Children's Chatting or something like that.

244. **David:** Yeah, it's like... (interrupted)

245. **Brian:** Microsoft's guide to what?

246. **David:** L33t speak.

247. **Brian:** Oh, ok.

248. **David:** It's like the Microsoft introduction to online gaming and how to help your kids get over gaming bullies and how to recognize what they're actually talking about.

249. **Brian:** I figured with SMS, there's all these abbreviations and stuff. Kids whose parents will buy them cell phones when they're like five or six for whatever reason, when they learn how to spell words correctly, they like, "Why would I ever spell it like that when

I can get the same word across in three characters?"
Yeah. It's screwing them up because of... (interrupted)

250. **Gavin:** The reduction of the language.
251. **Brian:** Yeah.
252. **David:** The new speak?
253. **Brian:** The new speak.
254. **David:** Plus not good(?)
255. **Gavin:** Enh... We'll just talk about <unintelligible>.
256. **Jay:** It's kind of opposite, though.
257. **Brian:** Yeah. There was a Family Guy where they have a brief... What was it? They're at a museum or something... Oh, they're at the laser show at a planetarium and they're like, "A quick demonstration of the binary language." And they're like, "We'll now do a play in binary." And, the woman is like, "Zero. Zero, zero, zero, one. Zero, zero, one, one, zero." It was pretty retarded, but funny nonetheless.
258. **David:** Family Guy's coming out in May.
259. **Brian:** Say what?
260. **David:** Family Guy on Fox in May. I look forward to that.
261. **Jay:** They should have brought back Futurama.
262. **Brian:** I feel like Family Guy is funnier.
263. **David:** I don't know. Futurama is... American Dad, I'm not so sure about that one.
264. **Gavin:** Futurama had so many scifi inside jokes that it was amazing.
265. **Brian:** Maybe that's why I didn't like it as much.

266. **Gavin:** You have to be a geeky scifi person.
267. **Brian:** Is the stuff that they show on the DVDs of Family Guy...? Is that uncensored? Do they really go that far?
268. **David:** Well, the Jew episode...
269. **Brian:** Which one?
270. **David:** When You Wish Upon a Weinstein.
271. **Brian:** Yeah, yeah. I saw that one the other day, and I was like, "Wow! Did they really show this on TV?"
272. **David:** Yeah. The song that Peter sings—"I know they didn't kill my lord" or whatever—and the DVD, it's "even though they killed my lord, I need a Jew."
273. **Brian:** Ah...
274. **David:** That's the end of the song. That's what... I don't know... I actually had it downloaded when they first played it on Cartoon Network. I played it simultaneously just to see what the difference was. It was pretty funny.
275. **Gavin:** It's not coming up. (Putting the computer away)
276. **David:** Unacceptable.
277. **Gavin:** Huh?
278. **David:** Unacceptable.
279. **Gavin:** Yeah, I know. Half the time, I have to hit the screen for the backlight to turn on.
280. **David:** I'm getting a laptop. It's in the mail. It should be at my house.
281. **Gavin:** Well, the most common fix is when these things start... when they, uh... (interrupted)

282. **Brian:** Contacts wear out?
283. **Gavin:** When the hinges start wearing out and they creak, it starts putting a torque on the LCD and it starts fracturing and stuff like that.
284. **Jay:** (Looking closely at the laptop) It looks like that hinge is cracking something awful.
285. **Gavin:** No, I… I had to disassemble it to grease up the hinges. So, it didn't come together quite right. Does anything ever come together quite right? "There's like five extra screws."

(long pause)

286. **Brian:** When Potts came here to talk, he stood right in front of the camera the whole time. I was like, "You're ruining their little project."
287. **Gavin:** Then, once David started speaking, he took notice and shifted to the side.
288. **Brian:** But, he stood there for five minutes, and I was like, "You're ruining this footage." But, I wasn't going to say anything. I thought it was kind of funny.
289. **Gavin:** No, I think he generally thought that he was obscuring David.
290. **David:** Just documenting a regular class discussion.
291. **Jay:** Yup. A regular day in the <unintelligible>

(long pause)

292. **Gavin:** <unintelligible>
293. **Brian:** Probably would if you said it.
294. **Gavin:** What's that?

295. **Brian:** Probably would if you said it. What kind of planes do they have there?

296. **Gavin:** It's the B-2s. That's the only place they fly out of in the <unintelligible>, except Diego Sierra when they were <unintelligible>.

297. **Jay:** Since we didn't have anyone doing an article presentation, are we just supposed to sit here in small groups for an hour and a half?

298. **Brian:** There's supposed to be a class discussion after this.

299. **David:** I'm thinking... (interrupted)

300. **Gavin:** There's just going to be more of the same thing.

301. **Jay:** There's only half an hour left in class, so what we can do is have a <unintelligible> discussion.

302. **Brian:** Yeah, because a big long group disc... (interrupted)

303. **Gavin:** <unintelligible>

304. **Brian:** "Everyone else just tries to copy." Is that it?

305. **Jay:** Yeah. We think anyone who publishes something on the Internet and expects it to be private... (interrupted)

306. **Brian:** And, there's always that one person that thinks of everything. "Well, actually... Blah, blah, blah."

307. **Gavin:** That's what I mean, someone always... (interrupted)

308. **Brian:** I really liked the guy last week <the guy who talked about privacy> because he shot a few kids down. He said stuff, and I was like "Get 'em." They're like, "No, of course, I can see my records

online from a doctor." He was like, "No, you can't."
He was like… I was like, "Get them."

(long pause)

309. **David:** God damn it. That guy over there, his laugh…
310. **Brian:** His what?
311. **David:** His greasy laugh. Go ahead and get that on tape. "I don't like his laugh."

(group laughs)
(laughter from another group)
(group laughs)

312. **David:** There it is again.
313. **Gavin:** <unintelligible>
314. **Brian:** So, now your parents can find out about what you said, and his parents are going to find out what you said. And, all of the other…
315. **David:** <unintelligible> team is everything.
316. **Brian:** He starts talking smack about the professor and stuff. "He said he would never find out. How was I supposed to know?" Invalidate all this kid's research.

(short pause while looking around)

317. **Brian:** Oh, that kid's also getting videotaped. They'll definitely know who you're talking about.
318. **Gavin:** Only if they run them simultaneously.
319. **Brian:** Well, if they have timestamps and stuff, it won't even be that hard.
320. **Jay:** I think he'll figure out who it is.

321. **David:** The researchers will get a kick out of that.
322. **Brian:** I'm sure they will. I hope they get a kick out of our whole conversation.
323. **Jay:** Some of the people haven't consented to participate, but notice that the camera is angled in that direction. That group is totally getting on film.
324. **Brian:** Maybe we should block them better.

(moves, Jim walks by)

325. **Brian:** Stay right there.
326. **David:** We need to get Ed back here.
327. **Brian:** What if we moon it?
328. **David:** "This is what happens in regular class discussions."
329. **Brian:** "I discuss best when naked. That's all I have to say." I saw that FaceBook had myParties as something that you could click on on the left in your profile, and I never noticed it before.
330. **David:** Really? That's definitely new.
331. **Brian:** So, I clicked on it, because I was like, "I don't have any parties. What do I have under here?" Apparently, I guess it's like stuff, events people have going on at Tech, and one of them was a streakfest. It said to meet at Britton wearing just an overcoat and that you continue on from there. I was like, "Who takes this seriously? Is anyone really going to show up?"
332. **David:** When it is?
333. **Brian:** It's like Saturday or something.
334. **David:** Damn it! (laughs)
335. **Brian:** And, then, it was like, "Click here for upcoming stuff" like… (interrupted)

336. **Gavin:** <unintelligible>.
337. **Brian:** Some kids have an orgy posted. I was just like, "This is completely silliness. This is never going to happen." No one is going to be like, "You know, I think I'm going to go to that" especially girls.
338. **Jay:** I don't know about that. Some of the people on my hall Freshman year were pretty nasty.
339. **Brian:** Yeah, I won't argue with that. I don't know... I was just like... Because, I thought of that, and you know how you have to have a name, so it would say who posted it. It's going to... I mean, your parents probably won't find out, but your friends will find out, and who knows who they'll tell. I don't know... I thought that was really... And faculty. You start like getting minors drunk and stuff, and they'll bust you big time.
340. **David:** Bill Leahy is one of my friend on FaceBook. He's got, apparently, not that many friends.
341. **Brian:** That's a bummer. John Goddard? I love John Goddard.
342. **David:** I know. He's awesome. I need to find him.
343. **Brian:** He was my... I had him for Java, 2200, and 2130.
344. **David:** I didn't have him for Java <unintelligible>
345. **Gavin:** <unintelligible> pseudocode and Java.
346. **Brian:** I had Jones for pseudocode.
347. **David:** I had him for Java, but for 2200, I had Goddard.
348. **Brian:** He was awesome in those classes.
349. **David:** That history stuff, that was great.

350. **Brian:** And, his little jokes… "Where do bits come from?" "Well, bits come from trees that grow…" It's just funny watching kids be like <acts like he's taking notes>. "I had no idea." Then, he was like, "No. Of course not." … And his little pictures. He got Britney Spears or the current hot chick of the day would somehow always be worked into one of his slides.

351. **Jay:** I know when I had him, Britney Spears, Christina Aguilera, and Chewbacca were on the slides.

352. **Brian:** Yeah, yeah, yeah. Exactly. Exactly. Or, when I took 2200, he had the PRS system. It was a test run. So, one day he shows up to class wearing this bright, bright yellow fleece vest, and someone said something about it… (interrupted)

353. **Jay:** I must have been in your class… (interrupted)

354. **Brian:** Yeah. Were you there?

355. **Jay:** Because I remember that…

356. **Brian:** Yeah. So, people start saying stuff, and he's like, "What do you guys think of the vest? What do you think of the vest?" He's like, "Alright, here's what we're going to do: nine if you really like it, zero if you hate it. Vote now." And, we just took like ten minutes voting on his vest. It was awesome.

(Ed ends the group discussions)

NOTES

1. In Chapter 3, I explore the implications of this design decision in more detail.
2. In addition to public self-awareness and private self-awareness, there is evidence for a *collective self-awareness* that involves how individuals perceive their roles relative to the goals of an important reference group (Crocker & Luhtanen, 1990). Based on collective self-awareness, research on social identity theory has found evidence that online environments can promote a greater sense of connection to the group, which reduces inhibition (Lea & Spears, 1991; Postmes & Spears, 1998; Spears, Lea, & Postmes, 2000, 2001).
3. In contradictory evidence, Rafal's (1996) case study of four girls co-constructing knowledge in a science classroom suggests that small groups generate relatively equal patterns of interaction, despite differences in academic social status among the participants. The group in this single case-study, however, was self-selected. As such, it is reasonable to assume that the previous relationships among these girls might have given them a sense of peer status unrelated to their academic status in whole-group discussions.
4. In psychological research, *proximal* variables refer to those with a simple, direct relationship to a dependent variable. *Distal* variables, however, influence intermediate—more proximal—variables, which, in turn, influence the dependent variable.
5. For a complete description of this procedure, see Guiora, Beit-Hallahmi, Brannon, Dull, and Scovel (1972).
6. Research in work-related settings has also found that online environments are unique, especially with regards to feelings of dominance and inhibition (e.g., Sproull & Kiesler, 1991).
7. In their research, Johnson and Johnson draw a sharp distinction between academic controversy as a specific type of group discussion and the more common "group discussion format." They state:

> In the "group discussion format," the instructor assigns students to small groups, gives them a question to discuss,

and facilitates (and moderates) as students exchange ideas, explain and elaborate their views, question and respond to each other, and jointly derive an answer. The questions tend to be open-ended and require higher-level cognitive reasoning to answer; the answers are open to interpretation. Knowledge is assumed to be dynamic and socially constructed. The instructor monitors the groups to facilitate discussion and obtain a "window" into students' minds by listening to their explanations. At its best, this format is cooperative learning; at its worst, it is traditional discussion groups. (Johnson, Johnson, & Smith, 2000, p. 30)

Johnson and Johnson, however, never compare academic controversy with less scripted forms of group discussion on a controversial topic.

8. A few studies on academic controversy (e.g., Mitchell, Johnson, & Johnson, 2002) conflated the concept of taking multiple perspectives with the notion of using different logical chains to support the same perspectives. Learning benefits observed in these studies, however, still emphasize the importance of elaboration on perspectives.

9. All names have been changed throughout this book.

10. Prior to becoming a language teacher, Prof. Sagnier had been a practicing architect in Paris. This was thus a subject that she found personally exciting.

11. Although the phrase *social loafing* more accurately refers to individuals who participate as little as possible in group settings, this body of research frequently considers questions of both negative motivational force (i.e., the impetus to minimize participation) and positive motivational force (i.e., the desire to participate fully).

12. One neighbor eventually called the police after the half-hour incident. Before doing so, however, he called a friend in another town for advice.

13. These studies are summarized with commentary in Latané and Darley (1970).

14. Throughout this section, *confederates* are students working for the research team who are trained not to respond. *Naïve* subjects are research subjects who are unaware of the nature of the study.

15. The psychological notion of self-awareness is divided into two types of awareness: public and private (Duval & Wicklund, 1972). Public self-awareness is an awareness that others (the public) are judging the actions of the individual. Private self-awareness occurs when an individual assesses his or her own performance. In the literature on disinhibition on the internet, only public self-awareness has been strongly correlated with online behavior (Matheson & Zanna, 1988). All references in this chapter to *self-awareness* only refer to *public self-awareness*. For a more complete description of self-awareness, refer to Chapter 2.

16. Note that these behavioral changes do not necessarily occur with all computer-supported collaborative learning (CSCL) technologies (Davis & Huttenlocher, 1995; Guzdial, 1997; Palonen & Hakkarainen, 2000; Guzdial et al., 2001; Guzdial & Carroll, 2002; Rick, Guzdial, Carroll, Holloway-Attaway, & Walker, 2002). Using the bystander effect can offer some insights into why researchers studying these environments have observed different participation patterns.

17. This course was originally a two credit-hour course numbered CS 4000. In the summer of 2003, it became a three credit-hour course numbered CS 4001.

18. An additional 19 students enrolled in a fifth section offered as part of a study abroad in New Zealand program.

19. Another class that I observed took place in a wide, but shallow room. (There were approximately 10 rows of 4 desks each going from the front of the room to the back). The students on the right side of the room tended to talk more than those in the back or to the left. Over the course of the semester, the instructor slowly changed her body language and stance to be more receptive to the right side of the room. By the end of the semester, she stood directly in front of this talkative group and rarely moved to the other side. When I later asked her about this, she was completely unaware that she had done it.

20. It is worth noting that, shortly before I began my research with CS 4001, the university decided to change the course length from two hours to three hours. This occurred largely because of the amount of course material.

21. The online/face-to-face schedule was designed to accommodate unrelated scheduling constraints.

22. The lost data included half of the Day 2 discussion for Group 2, all of the Day 2 discussion for Group 4, all of the Day 4 discussion for Group 5, and all of the Day 4 discussion for Group 7.

23. During my pilot studies, I observed a number of small group discussions (both online and in the face-to-face classroom). From these observations, I discovered that students rarely advocate contradictory positions. Instead, they typically engage in something more akin to joint problem solving. Although the students briefly "try on" positions by advocating them, it seems that they are simply testing a given perspective in order to understand its validity.

24. The implications of this decision are described in more detail in the next section, which focuses on converting the aggregated argument list into a quantifiable "grade."

25. Note that throughout this section, I use Times New Roman font for face-to-face discussion and Courier font for online discussions.

26. Because of the number of factors that vary for each data point (i.e., media condition, number of group members, instructor attention, etc.), a hierarchical linear regression model would provide a better statistical analysis. Unfortunately, there are not enough data points in this study for this type of model to have sufficient statistical power. Similarly, the T-tests described here have only limited statistical power and represent trends in the data.

27. A couple of questions have been combined because the student groups discussed these questions together. It is impossible to separate answers to one question from answers to the other.

REFERENCES

Allen, I. E., & Seaman, J. (2003). *Sizing the Opportunity: The Quality and Extent of Online Education in the United States, 2002 and 2003*: The Sloan Consortium.

Allen, I. E., & Seaman, J. (2004). *Entering the Mainstream: The Quality and Extent of Online Education in the United States, 2003 and 2004*: The Sloan Consortium.

Allen, M., Mabry, E., Mattrey, M., Bourhis, J., Titsworth, S., & Burrell, N. (2004). Evaluating the Effectiveness of Distance Learning: A Comparison Using Meta-Analysis. *Journal of Communication, 54* (3), 402–420.

Anderson, C., John, O. P., Keltner, D., & Kring, A. M. (2001). Who Attains Social Status? Effects of Personality and Physical Attractiveness in Social Groups. *Journal of Personality and Social Psychology, 81* (1), 116–132.

Andriessen, J. (2006). Arguing to Learn. In R. K. Sawyer (Ed.), *The Cambridge Handbook of the Learning Sciences*. Cambridge: Cambridge University Press.

Andriessen, J., Erkens, G., van de Laak, C., Peters, N., & Coirier, P. (2003). Argumentation as Negotiation in Electronic Collaborative Writing. In J. Andriessen, M. Baker & D. Suthers (Eds.), *Arguing to Learn: Confronting Cognitions in Computer-Supported Collaborative Learning Environments* (pp. 79–116). Dordrecht: Kluwer Academic Publishers.

Asch, S. (1951). Effects of Group Pressure upon the Modification and Distortion of Judgments. In H. Guetzkow (Ed.), *Groups, Leadership, and Men* (pp. 177–190). Pittsburgh, PA: Carnegie Press.

Asch, S. (1956). Studies of Independence and Submission to Group Pressure I: On Minority of One against Unanimous Majority. *Psychological Monographs, 70* (10).

Baker, M. (2003). Computer-Mediated Argumentative Interactions for the Co-Elaboration of Scientific Notions. In J. Andriessen, M. Baker & D. Suthers (Eds.), *Arguing to Learn: Confronting Cognitions in Computer-Supported Collaborative Learning Environments* (pp. 47–78). Dordrecht: Kluwer Academic Publishers.

Bargh, J. A., McKenna, K. Y. A., & Fitzsimons, G. M. (2002). Can You See the Real Me? Activation and Expression of the "True Self" on the Internet. *Journal of Social Issues, 58* (1), 33–48.

Barron, B. (2003). When Smart Groups Fail. *Journal of the Learning Sciences, 12* (3), 307–359.

Batson, T. (1993). The Origins of ENFI. In B. Bruce, J. K. Peyton & T. Batson (Eds.), *Network-Based Classrooms: Promises and Realities* (pp. 87–112). Cambridge: Cambridge University Press.

Baumeister, R. F. (1984). Choking Under Pressure: Self-Consciousness and Paradoxical Effects of Incentives on Skillful Performance. *Journal of Personality and Social Psychology, 46* (3), 610–620.

Beauvois, M. H. (1992a). *Computer-Assisted Classroom Discussion in French Using Networked Computers.* Unpublished Ph.D. Dissertation, University of Texas at Austin, Austin, TX.

Beauvois, M. H. (1992b). Computer-Assisted Classroom Discussion in the Foreign Language Classroom: Conversation in Slow Motion. *Foreign Language Annals, 25* (5), 455–464.

Beauvois, M. H. (1994/1995). E-Talk: Attitudes and Motivation in Computer-Assisted Classroom Discussion. *Computers and the Humanities, 28* (3), 177–190.

Beauvois, M. H. (1997). Computer-Mediated Communication (CMC): Technology for Improving Speaking and Writing. In M. D. Bush & R. M. Terry (Eds.), *Technology-Enhanced Language Learning* (pp. 165–184). Lincolnwood: National Textbook Company.

Beauvois, M. H., & Eledge, J. (1995/1996). Personality Types and Mega-bytes: Student Attitudes Toward Computer Mediated Communication (CMC) in the Language Classroom. *CALICO Journal, 13* (2&3), 27–45.

Bell, P., Davis, E., & Linn, M. C. (1995). The Knowledge Integration Environment: Theory and Design. In *Proceedings of the Conference on Computer Support for Collaborative Learning (CSCL)* (pp. 14–21). Bloomington, IN.

Bernard, R. M., Abrami, P. C., Lou, Y., & Borokhovski, E. (2004). A Methodological Morass? How We Can Improve Quantitative Research in Distance Education. *Distance Education, 25* (2), 175–198.

Bernard, R. M., Abrami, P. C., Lou, Y., Borokhovski, E., Wade, A., Wozney, L., et al. (2004). How Does Distance Education Compare with Classroom Instruction? A Meta-Analysis of the Empirical Literature. *Review of Educational Research, 74* (3), 379–439.

Bond, C. F., & Titus, L. J. (1983). Social Facilitation: A Meta-Analysis of 241 Studies. *Psychological Bulletin, 94* (2), 265–292.

Brown, A. L. (1992). Design Experiments: Theoretical and Methodological Challenges in Creating Complex Interventions in Classroom Settings. *The Journal of the Learning Sciences, 2* (2), 141–178.

Bruce, B. C., Peyton, J. K., & Batson, T. (Eds.). (1993). *Network-Based Classrooms: Promises and Realities.* New York, NY: Cambridge University Press.

Bruckman, A. (1999). The Day After Net Day: Approaches to Educational Use of the Internet. *Convergence, 5* (1), 24–46.

Callahan, D. (1980). Goals in the Teaching of Ethics. In D. Callahan & S. Bok (Eds.), *Ethics Teaching in Higher Education* (pp. 61–80). New York, NY: Plenum Press.

Callahan, D., & Bok, S. (1980). *Ethics Teaching in Higher Education.* New York: Plenum Press.

Cherny, L. (1999). *Conversation and Community: Chat in a Virtual World.* Stanford: CSLI Publications.

Chi, M. T. H., Feltovich, P. J., & Glaser, R. (1981). Categorization and Representation of Physics Problems by Experts and Novices. *Cognitive Science, 5* (2), 121–152.

Chizhik, A. W. (1999). Can Students Work Together Equitably? An Analysis of Task Effects in Collaborative Group Work. *Social Psychology of Education, 3* (1), 63–79.

Chizhik, A. W. (2001). Equity and Status in Group Collaboration: Learning Through Explanations Depends on Task Characteristics. *Social Psychology of Education, 5* (2), 179–200.

Churchill, E., Trevor, J., Bly, S., & Nelson, L. (2000). StickyChats: Remote Conversations over Digital Documents. In *Proceedings of the 2000 Conference on Computer Supported Cooperative Work (CSCW)* (Vol. Video Program, pp. 350). Philadelphia, PA: ACM Press.

Clarkson, E., Clawson, J., Lyons, K., & Starner, T. (2005). An Empirical Study of Typing Rates on mini-QWERTY Keyboards. In *Extended Abstracts of Human Factors in Computing (CHI)* (pp. 1288–1291). Portland, OR: ACM Press.

Cohen, A., & Scardamalia, M. (1998). Discourse About Ideas: Monitoring and Regulation in Face-to-Face and Computer-Mediated Environments. *Interactive Learning Environments, 6* (1–2), 93–113.

Cohen, E. G. (1984). Talking and Working Together: Status Interaction and Learning. In P. Peterson, L. C. Wilkinson & M. Hallinan (Eds.), *Instructional Groups in the Classroom: Organization and Processes* (pp. 171–188). Orlando, FL: Academic.

Cohen, E. G. (1994). Restructuring the Classroom: Conditions for Productive Small Groups. *Review of Educational Research, 64* (1), 1–35.

Cohen, E. G., & Lotan, R. A. (1995). Producing Equal-Status Interaction in the Heterogeneous Classroom. *American Educational Research Journal, 32* (1), 99–120.

Cohen, E. G., Lotan, R. A., Scarloss, B. A., & Arellano, A. R. (1999). Complex Instruction: Equity in Cooperative Learning Classrooms. *Theory Into Practice, 38* (2), 80–86.

Collison, G., Elbaum, B., Haavind, S., & Tinker, R. (2000). *Facilitating Online Learning: Effective Strategies for Moderators*. Madison, WI: Atwood Publishing.

Collot, M., & Belmore, N. (1996). Electronic Language: A New Variety of English. In S. C. Herring (Ed.), *Computer-Mediated Communication: Linguistic, Social and Cross-Cultural Perspectives* (pp. 13–28). Philadelphia, PA: John Benjamins Publishing Co.

Condon, S. L., & Cech, C. G. (1996). Functional Comparisons of Face-to-Face and Computer-Mediated Decisions Making Interactions. In S. C. Herring (Ed.), *Computer-Mediated Communication: Linguistic, Social, and Cross-Cultural Perspectives* (pp. 65–80). Philadelphia, PA: John Benjamins Publishing Company.

Crocker, J., & Luhtanen, R. (1990). Collective Self-Esteem and Ingroup Bias. *Journal of Personality and Social Psychology, 58* (1), 60–67.

Cuban, L. (2001). *Oversold and Underused: Computers in the Classroom.* Cambridge, MA: Harvard University Press.

Daniel, J. S. (1996). *Mega-Universities and the Knowledge Media: Technology Strategies for Higher Education.* London, England: Kogan Page.

Darley, J. M., & Latané, B. (1968). Bystander Intervention in Emergencies: Diffusion of Responsibility. *Journal of Personality and Social Psychology, 8* (4), 377–383.

Darragh, J. J., & Witten, I. H. (1992). *The Reactive Keyboard.* New York, NY: Cambridge University Press.

Davis, J. R., & Huttenlocher, D. P. (1995). Shared Annotation for Cooperative Learning. In *Proceedings of Computer Supported Collaborative Learning (CSCL) 1995* (pp. 84–88). Bloomington, IN: Lawrence Erlbaum Associates.

de Vries, E., Lund, K., & Baker, M. (2002). Computer-Mediated Epistemic Dialogue: Explanation and Argumentation as Vehicles for Understanding Scientific Notions. *Journal of the Learning Sciences, 11* (1), 63–103.

Dembo, M. H., & McAuliffe, T. J. (1987). Effects of Perceived Ability and Grade Status on Social Interaction and Influence in Cooperative Groups. *Journal of Educational Psychology, 79* (4), 415–423.

Dery, M. (Ed.). (1993). *Flame Wars: The Discourse of Cyberculture.* Durham, NC: Duke University Press.

Dillenbourg, P. (2002). Over-Scripting CSCL: The Risks of Blending Collaborative Learning with Instructional Design. In P. A. Kirschner (Ed.), *Three Worlds of CSCL: Can we Support CSCL?* (pp. 61–91). Heerlen: Open Universiteit Nederland.

DiMicco, J. M., Pandolfo, A., & Bender, W. (2004). Influencing Group Participation with a Shared Display. In *Proceeding of the 2004 Conference on Computer-Supported Cooperative Work (CSCW)* (pp. 614–627). Chicago, IL: ACM Press.

Dubrovsky, V. J., Kiesler, S., & Sethna, B. N. (1991). The Equalization Phenomenon: Status Effects in Computer-Mediated and Face-to-Face Decision Making Groups. *Human Computer Interaction, 6* (2), 119–146.

Duval, S., & Wicklund, R. A. (1972). *A Theory of Objective Self Awareness*. New York, NY: Academic Press.

Engeström, Y., Miettinen, R., & Punamäki, R.-L. (Eds.). (1999). *Perspectives on Activity Theory*. New York, NY: Cambridge University Press.

Erickson, T., Halverson, C., Kellogg, W. A., Laff, M., & Wolf, T. (2002). Social Translucence: Designing Social Infrastructures that Make Collective Activity Visible. *Communications of the ACM, 45* (4), 40–44.

Erickson, T., & Kellogg, W. A. (2000). Social Translucence: An Approach to Designing Systems that Support Social Processes. *ACM Transactions on Computer-Human Interaction, 7* (1), 59–83.

Farnham, S., Chesley, H. R., McGhee, D. E., Kawal, R., & Landau, J. (2000). Structured Online Interactions: Improving the Decision-Making of Small Discussion Groups. In *Proceedings of the 2000 Conference on Computer Supported Cooperative Work (CSCW)* (pp. 299–308). Philadelphia, PA: ACM Press.

Fenigstein, A., Scheier, M. F., & Buss, A. H. (1975). Public and Private Self-Consciousness: Assessment and Theory. *Journal of Consulting and Clinical Psychology, 43* (4), 522–527.

Festinger, L. (1957). *A Theory of Cognitive Dissonance*. Stanford, CA: Stanford University Press.

Fjermestad, J., & Hiltz, S. R. (1998–1999). An Assessment of Group Support Systems Experimental Research: Methodology and Results. *Journal of Management Information Systems, 15* (3), 7–149.

France, E. F., Anderson, A. H., & Gardner, M. (2001). The Impact of Status and Audio Conferencing Technology on Business Meetings. *International Journal of Human-Computer Studies, 54* (6), 857–876.

Freiermuth, M. R. (2001). Native Speakers or Non-Native Speakers: Who Has the Floor? Online and Face-to-Face Interaction in Culturally Mixed Small Groups. *Computer Assisted Language Learning, 14* (2), 169–199.

Galvin, T. (2002). 2002 Industry Report. *Training, 39* (10), 24–48.

Geen, R. G. (1991). Social Motivation. *Annual Review of Psychology, 43* (1), 377–399.

Glaser, B. G., & Strauss, A. L. (1967). *The Discovery of Grounded Theory: Strategies for Qualitative Research.* Chicago, IL: Aldine Publishing Company.

Goffman, E. (1959). *The Presentation of Self in Everyday Life.* New York: Doubleday.

Goffman, E. (1963). *Behavior in Public Places: Notes on the Social Organization of Gatherings.* New York, NY: The Free Press.

Goffman, E. (1967). *Interaction Ritual: Essays on Face-to-Face Behavior.* New York, NY: Pantheon Books.

Greenberg, J., & Pyszczynski, T. (1986). Persistent High Self-Focus After Failure and Low Self-Focus After Success: The Depressive Self-Focusing Style. *Journal of Personality and Social Psychology, 50* (5), 1039–1044.

Grice, H. P. (1975). Logic and Conversation. In P. Cole & J. Mordan (Eds.), *Syntax and Semantics* (Vol. 3, pp. 41–58). New York, NY: Academic Press.

Guiora, A. Z. (1972). Construct Validity and Transpositional Research: Toward an Empirical Study of Psychoanalytic Concepts. *Comprehensive Psychiatry, 13* (2), 139–150.

Guiora, A. Z., Acton, W. R., Erard, R., & Strickland, F. W. (1980). The Effects of Benzodiazepine (Valium) on Permeability of Language Ego Boundaries. *Language Learning, 30* (2), 351–363.

Guiora, A. Z., Beit-Hallahmi, B., Brannon, R. C. L., Dull, C. Y., & Scovel, T. (1972). The Effects of Experimentally Induced Changes in Ego States on Pronunciation Ability in a Second Language: An Exploratory Study. *Comprehensive Psychiatry, 13* (5), 421–428.

Guzdial, M. (1997). Information Ecology of Collaborations in Educational Settings: Influence of Tool. In *Proceedings of Computer Supported Collaborative Learning (CSCL) 1997* (pp. 83–91). Toronto, Canada: Lawrence Erlbaum Associates.

Guzdial, M., & Carroll, K. (2002). Exploring the Lack of Dialog in Computer-Supported Collaborative Learning. In *Proceedings of Computer-Supported Collaborative Learning (CSCL) 2002* (pp. 418–424). Boulder, CO: Lawrence Erlbaum Associates.

Guzdial, M., Ludovice, P., Realff, M., Morley, T., Carroll, K., & Ladak, A. (2001). The Challenge of Collaboration in Math and Engineering. In *Proceedings of IEEE/ASEE Frontiers in Education 2001* (pp. 23–28). Reno, NV: IEEE.

Guzdial, M., & Turns, J. (2000). Effective Discussion Through a Computer-Mediated Anchored Forum. *Journal of the Learning Sciences, 9* (4), 437–469.

Habermas, J. (1962). *The Structural Transformation of the Public Sphere: An Inquiry into a Category of Bourgeois Society* (T. Burger & F. Lawrence, Trans.). Cambridge, MA: MIT Press.

Habermas, J. (1990). *Moral Consciousness and Communicative Action* (C. Lenhardt & S. W. Nicholsen, Trans.). Cambridge, MA: MIT Press.

Habermas, J. (1993). *Justification and Application: Remarks on Discourse Ethics* (C. P. Cronin, Trans.). Cambridge, MA: MIT Press.

Haythornthwaite, C. (2002). Building Social Networks Via Computer Networks: Creating and Sustaining Distributed Learning Communities. In K. A. Renninger & W. Shumar (Eds.), *Building Virtual Communities: Learning and Change in Cyberspace* (pp. 159–190). New York, NY: Cambridge University Press.

Haythornthwaite, C., & Kazmer, M. M. (Eds.). (2004). *Learning, Culture, and Community in Online Education: Research and Practice.* New York, NY: Peter Lang.

Herring, S. (1999). Interactional Coherence in CMC. *Journal of Computer-Mediated Communication, 4* (4), http://jcmc.indiana.edu/vol4/issue4/herring.html.

Hiltz, S. R., & Turoff, M. (1978). *The Network Nation: Human Communication via Computer*. Reading, MA: Addison-Wesley Publishing.

Hsi, S., & Hoadley, C. M. (1997). Productive Discussion in Science: Gender Equity through Electronic Discourse. *Journal of Science Education and Technology, 6* (1), 23–36.

Huang, W., Olson, J. S., & Olson, G. M. (2002). Camera Angle Affects Dominance in Video-Mediated Communication. In *Proceedings of Human Factors in Computing (CHI) 2002* (pp. 716–717). Minneapolis, MN: ACM Press.

Hudson, J. M., & Bruckman, A. (2001). Effects of CMC on Student Participation Patterns in a Foreign Language Learning Environment. In *Proceedings of the 2001 Conference on Human Factors in Computing (CHI)* (pp. 263–264). Seattle, WA: ACM Press.

Hudson, J. M., & Bruckman, A. (2002). IRC Français: The Creation of an Internet-based SLA Community. *Computer Assisted Language Learning, 15* (2), 109–134.

Hudson, J. M., & Bruckman, A. (2004). The Bystander Effect: A Lens for Understanding Patterns of Participation. *Journal of the Learning Sciences, 13* (2), 169–199.

Jermann, P., & Dillenbourg, P. (2003). Elaborating New Arguments through a CSCL Script. In J. Andriessen, M. Baker & D. Suthers (Eds.), *Arguing to Learn: Confronting Cognitions in Computer-Supported Collaborative Learning Environments* (pp. 205–226). Dordrecht: Kluwer Academic Publishers.

Job-Sluder, K., & Barab, S. A. (2004). Shared "We" and Shared "They" Indicators of Group Identity in Online Teacher Professional Development. In S. A. Barab, R. Kling & J. H. Gray (Eds.), *Designing for Virtual Communities in the Service of Learning* (pp. 338–376). New York, NY: Cambridge University Press.

Johnson, D. W., & Johnson, R. T. (1988). Critical Thinking Through Structured Controversy. *Educational Leadership, 45* (8), 58–64.

Johnson, D. W., & Johnson, R. T. (2000). Civil Political Discourse in a Democracy: The Contribution of Psychology. *Peace and Conflict: Journal of Peace Psychology, 6* (4), 291–317.

Johnson, D. W., Johnson, R. T., & Smith, K. A. (2000). Constructive Controversy: The Educative Power of Intellectual Conflict. *Change, 32* (1), 28–37.

Joinson, A. N. (1998). Causes and Implications of Disinhibited Behavior on the Internet. In J. Gackenbach (Ed.), *Psychology and the Internet: Intrapersonal, Interpersonal, and Transpersonal Implications* (pp. 43–60). San Diego: Academic Press.

Joinson, A. N. (2001a). "Knowing Me, Knowing You": Reciprocal Self-Disclosure and Internet-Based Surveys. *Cyberpsychology and Behavior, 4* (5), 587–591.

Joinson, A. N. (2001b). Self-Disclosure in Computer-Mediated Communication: The Role of Self-Awareness and Visual Anonymity. *European Journal of Social Psychology, 31* (2), 177–192.

Joinson, A. N. (2003). *Understanding the Psychology of Internet Behavior: Virtual Worlds, Real Lives.* New York, NY: Palgrave Macmillan.

Kanazawa, S., & Kovar, J. L. (2004). Why Beautiful People are More Intelligent. *Intelligence, 32* (3), 227–243.

Karau, S. J., & Williams, K. D. (1993). Social Loafing: A Meta-Analytic Review and Theoretical Integration. *Journal of Personality and Social Psychology, 65* (4), 681–706.

Keefer, M., & Ashley, K. D. (2001). Case-based Approaches to Professional Ethics: A Systematic Comparison of Students' and Ethicists' Moral Reasoning. *Journal of Moral Education, 30* (4), 377–398.

Keefer, M. W., Zeitz, C. M., & Resnick, L. B. (2000). Judging the Quality of Peer-Led Student Dialogues. *Cognition and Instruction, 18* (1), 53–81.

Kelm, O. R. (1992). The Use of Synchronous Computer Networks in Second Language Instruction: A Preliminary Report. *Foreign Language Annals, 25* (5), 441–454.

Kern, R. G. (1995). Restructuring Classroom Interaction with Networked Computers: Effects on Quantity and Characteristics of Language Production. *Modern Language Journal, 79* (4), 457–476.

Kiesler, S., & Cummings, J. N. (2002). What Do We Know about Proximity and Distance in Work Groups? A Legacy of Research. In P. J. Hinds &

S. Kiesler (Eds.), *Distributed Work* (pp. 57–82). Cambridge, MA: MIT Press.

Kiesler, S., Siegel, J., & McGuire, T. W. (1984). Social Psychological Aspects of Computer-Mediated Communication. *American Psychologist, 39* (10), 1123–1134.

Kollock, P. (1999). The Economies of Online Cooperation: Gifts and Public Goods in Cyberspace. In M. A. Smith & P. Kollock (Eds.), *Communities in Cyberspace* (pp. 220–238). New York, NY: Routledge.

Kollock, P., & Smith, M. (1996). Managing the Virtual Commons: Cooperation and Conflict in Computer Communities. In S. C. Herring (Ed.), *Computer-Mediated Communication: Linguistic, Social, and Cross-Cultural Perspectives* (pp. 109–128). Philadelphia, PA: John Benjamins Publishing Company.

Kolodner, J. L. (1997). Educational Implications of Analogy: A View From Case-Based Reasoning. *American Psychologist, 52* (1), 57–66.

Kolodner, J. L., Camp, P. J., Crismond, D., Fasse, B., Gray, J., Holbrook, J., et al. (2003). Problem-Based Learning Meets Case-Based Reasoning in the Middle-School Science Classroom: Putting Learning by Design Into Practice. *Journal of the Learning Sciences, 12* (4), 495–547.

Kolodner, J. L., & Gray, J. (2002). Understanding the Affordances of Ritualized Activity Structures for Project-Based Classrooms. In *Proceedings of the International Conference on the Learning Sciences* (pp. 221–228). Seattle, WA: Lawrence Erlbaum.

Kraut, R. E., Fussell, S. R., Brennan, S. E., & Siegel, J. (2002). Understanding Effects of Proximity on Collaboration: Implications for Technologies to Support Remote Collaborative Work. In P. J. Hinds & S. Kiesler (Eds.), *Distributed Work* (pp. 137–164). Cambridge, MA: MIT Press.

Latané, B. (1970). Field Studies in Altruistic Compliance. *Representative Research in Social Psychology, 1* (1), 49–61.

Latané, B., & Darley, J. M. (1968). Group Inhibition of Bystander Intervention in Emergencies. *Journal of Personality and Social Psychology, 10* (3), 215–221.

Latané, B., & Darley, J. M. (1969). Bystander "Apathy." *American Scientist, 57,* 244–268.

Latané, B., & Darley, J. M. (1970). *The Unresponsive Bystander: Why Doesn't He Help?* New York, NY: Appleton-Century-Crofts.

Latané, B., & Rodin, J. (1969). A Lady in Distress: Inhibiting Effects of Friends and Strangers on Bystander Intervention. *Journal of Experimental Social Psychology, 5,* 189–202.

Lea, M., & Spears, R. (1991). Computer-Mediated Communication, De-Individuation, and Group Decision-Making. *International Journal of Man-Machine Studies, 34* (2), 283–301.

Lease, A. M., Musgrove, K. T., & Axelrod, J. L. (2002). Dimensions of Social Status in Preadolescent Peer Groups: Likability, Perceived Popularity, and Social Dominance. *Social Development, 11* (4), 508–533.

Levine, J. M., & Moreland, R. L. (1998). Small Groups. In D. T. Gilbert, S. T. Fiske & G. Lindzey (Eds.), *The Handbook of Social Psychology* (4th ed., pp. 415–469). New York, NY: McGraw-Hill.

Lloyd, P., & Cohen, E. G. (1999). Peer Status in the Middle School: A Natural Treatment for Unequal Participation. *Social Psychology of Education, 3* (3), 193–216.

Lou, Y., Abrami, P. C., & d'Apollonia, S. (2001). Small Group and Individual Learning with Technology: A Meta-Analysis. *Review of Educational Research, 71* (3), 449–521.

Margolis, J., & Fisher, A. (2002). *Unlocking the Clubhouse: Women in Computing.* Cambridge, MA: MIT Press.

Markey, P. M. (2000). Bystander Intervention in Computer-Mediated Communication. *Computers in Human Behavior, 16* (2), 183–188.

Matheson, K., & Zanna, M. P. (1988). The Impact of Computer-Mediated Communication on Self-Awareness. *Computers in Human Behavior, 4* (3), 221–233.

McDaniel, S. E., Olson, G. M., & Magee, J. C. (1996). Identifying and Analyzing Multiple Threads in Computer-Mediated and Face-to-Face Conversations. In *Proceedings of the 1996 Conference on Computer Supported Cooperative Work (CSCW)* (pp. 39–47). Boston, MA: ACM Press.

Merchant, G. (2001). Teenagers in Cyberspace: An Investigation of Language Use and Language Change in Internet Chatrooms. *Journal of Research in Reading, 24* (3), 293–306.

Mistler-Jackson, M., & Songer, N. B. (2000). Student Motivation and Internet Technology: Are Students Empowered to Learn Science? *Journal of Research in Science Teaching, 37* (5), 459–479.

Mitchell, J. M., Johnson, D. W., & Johnson, R. T. (2002). Are All Types of Cooperation Equal? Impace of Academic Controversy Versus Concurrence Seeking on Health Education. *Social Psychology of Education, 5* (4), 329–344.

Nardi, B. A., & Whittaker, S. (2002). The Place of Face-to-Face Communication in Distributed Work. In P. J. Hinds & S. Kiesler (Eds.), *Distributed Work* (pp. 83–112). Cambridge, MA: MIT Press.

Nasir, N. S. (2005). Individual Cognitive Structuring and the Sociocultural Context: Strategy Shifts in the Game of Dominoes. *Journal of the Learning Sciences, 14* (1), 5–34.

Newman, D., Griffin, P., & Cole, M. (1989). *The Construction Zone: Working for Cognitive Change in School*. New York: Cambridge University Press.

Nye, B., Hedges, L. V., & Konstantopoulos, S. (2004). Do Minorities Experience Larger Lasting Benefits from Small Classes? *Journal of Educational Research, 98* (2), 94–100.

O'Donnell, A. M., & Dansereau, D. F. (1992). Scripted Cooperation in Student Dyads: A Method for Analyzing and Enhancing Academic Learning. In R. Hertz-Lazarowitz & N. Miller (Eds.), *Interaction in Cooperative Groups: The Theoretical Anatomy of Group Learning* (pp. 120–141). New York, NY: Cambridge University Press.

Oikarinen, J. (n.d.). IRC History (http://www.irc.org/history_docs/jarkko. html). Retrieved October 27, 2005

Olson, J. S., Teasley, S., Covi, L., & Olson, G. (2002). The (Currently) Unique Advantages of Collocated Work. In P. J. Hinds & S. Kiesler (Eds.), *Distributed Work* (pp. 113–136). Cambridge, MA: MIT Press.

Ornstein, R., & Ehrlich, P. (1989). *New World New Mind: Moving Toward Conscious Evolution*. New York, NY: Doubleday.

Ortega, L. (1997). Processes and Outcomes in Networked Classroom Interaction: Defining the Research Agenda for L2 Computer-Assisted Classroom Discussion. *Language Learning and Technology, 1* (1), 82–93.

Palincsar, A. S., & Brown, A. L. (1984). Reciprocal Teaching of Comprehension-Fostering and Comprehension-Monitoring Activities. *Cognition and Instruction, 1* (2), 117–175.

Palonen, T., & Hakkarainen, K. (2000). Patterns of Interaction in Computer-Supported Learning: A Social Network Analysis. In *Fourth International Conference of the Learning Sciences (ICLS) 2000* (pp. 334–339). Ann Arbor, MI: Erlbaum.

Payne, J. S., & Ross, B. M. (2005). Synchronous CMC, Working Memory, and L2 Oral Proficiency Development. *Language Learning and Technology, 9* (3), 35–54.

Payne, J. S., & Whitney, P. J. (2002). Developing L2 Oral Proficiency Through Synchronous CMC: Output, Working Memory, and Interlanguage Development. *CALICO Journal, 20* (1), 7–32.

Pellettieri, J. (2000). Negotiation in Cyberspace: The Role of Chatting in the Development of Grammatical Competence. In M. Warschauer & R. Kern (Eds.), *Network-based Language Teaching: Concepts and Practice* (pp. 59–86). New York: Cambridge University Press.

Pintrich, P. R., & Schunk, D. H. (1996). *Motivation in Education: Theory, Research, and Applications.* Englewood Cliffs, NJ: Merrill.

Postmes, T., & Spears, R. (1998). Deindividuation and Antinormative Behavior: A Meta-Analysis. *Psychological Bulletin, 123* (3), 238–259.

Prentice-Dunn, S., & Rogers, R. W. (1982). Effects of Public and Private Self-Awareness on Deindividuation and Aggression. *Journal of Personality and Social Psychology, 43* (3), 503–513.

Rafal, C. T. (1996). From Co-Construction to Takeovers: Science Talk in a Group of Four Girls. *Journal of the Learning Sciences, 5* (3), 279–293.

Resnick, L. B., Salmon, M., Zeitz, C. M., Wathen, S. H., & Holowchak, M. (1993). Reasoning in Conversation. *Cognition and Instruction, 11* (3&4), 347–364.

Rheingold, H. (1993). *The Virtual Community: Homesteading on the Electronic Frontier.* New York: HarperCollins.

Rick, J., Guzdial, M., Carroll, K., Holloway-Attaway, L., & Walker, B. (2002). Collaborative Learning at Low Cost: CoWeb Use in English Composition. In *Proceedings of Computer Supported Collaborative Learning (CSCL) 2002* (pp. 435–442). Boulder, CO.

Rosenthal, A. M. (1964/1999). *Thirty-Eight Witnesses: The Kitty Genovese Case*. Berkeley, CA: University of California Press.

Salomon, G. (Ed.). (1993). *Distributed Cognitions: Psychological and Educational Considerations*. New York, NY: Cambridge University Press.

Sassenberg, K. (2002). Common Bond and Common Identity Groups on the Internet: Attachment and Normative Behavior in On-Topic and Off-Topic Chats. *Group Dynamics: Theory, Research, and Practice, 6* (1), 27–37.

Schön, D. A. (1987). *Educating the Reflective Practitioner*. San Francisco: Jossey-Bass.

Schumann, J. H., Holroyd, J., Campbell, R. N., & Ward, F. A. (1978). Improvement of Foreign Language Pronunciation Under Hypnosis. *Language Learning, 28* (1), 143–148.

Schwarz, B. B., & Glassner, A. (2003). The Blind and the Paralytic: Supporting Argumentation in Everyday and Scientific Issues. In J. Andriessen, M. Baker & D. Suthers (Eds.), *Arguing to Learn: Confronting Cognitions in Computer-Supported Collaborative Learning Environments* (pp. 227–260). Dordrecht: Kluwer Academic Publishers.

Scovel, T. (2000). A Critical Review of the Critical Period Research. *Annual Review of Applied Linguistics, 20* (1), 213–223.

Setzer, J. C., Lewis, L., & Greene, B. (2005). *Distance Education Courses for Public Elementary and Secondary School Students: 2002–03 (NCES 2005–010)*: U.S. Department of Education, National Center for Educational Statistics.

Silvia, P. J., & Duval, T. S. (2001). Objective Self-Awareness Theory: Recent Progress and Enduring Problems. *Personality and Social Psychology Review, 5* (3), 230–241.

Simpson, J. (2005). Conversational Floors in Synchronous Text-Based CMC Discourse. *Discourse Studies, 7* (3), 337–361.

Smith, K. A., Johnson, D. W., & Johnson, R. T. (1984). Effects of Controversy on Learning in Cooperative Groups. *The Journal of Social Psychology, 122* (2), 199–209.

Smith, K. A., Petersen, R. P., Johnson, D. W., & Johnson, R. T. (1986). The Effects of Controversy and Concurrence Seeking on Effective Decision Making. *The Journal of Social Psychology, 126* (2), 237–248.

Smith, M., Cadiz, J., & Burkhalter, B. (2002). Conversation Trees and Threaded Chats. In *Proceedings of the 2002 Conference on Computer Supported Cooperative Work (CSCW)* (pp. 97–105). New Orleans, LA: ACM Press.

Songer, N. (1996). Exploring Learning Opportunities in Coordinated Network-Enhanced Classrooms: A Case of Kids as Global Scientists. *Journal of the Learning Sciences, 5* (4), 297–327.

Spears, R., Lea, M., & Postmes, T. (2000). On SIDE: Purview, Problems, and Prospects. In T. Postmes, R. Spears, M. Lea & S. D. Reicher (Eds.), *SIDE Issues Centre Stage: Recent Developments of Deindividuation in Groups* (pp. 1–16). Amsterdam: KNAW.

Spears, R., Lea, M., & Postmes, T. (2001). Social Psychological Theories of Computer-Mediated Communication: Social Pain or Social Gain? In W. P. Robinson & H. Giles (Eds.), *The New Handbook of Language and Social Psychology (Second Edition)* (pp. 601–624). New York, NY: John Wiley and Sons.

Sproull, L., & Kiesler, S. (1991). *Connections: New Ways of Working in the Networked Organization.* Cambridge: MIT Press.

Steiner, I. D. (1972). *Group Process and Productivity.* New York, NY: Academic Press.

Stevahn, L., Johnson, D. W., Johnson, R. T., & Schultz, R. (2002). Effects of Conflict Resolution Training Integrated Into a High School Social Studies Curriculum. *The Journal of Social Psychology, 142* (3), 305–331.

Strauss, A. L., & Corbin, J. M. (1998). *Basics of Qualitative Research: Techniques and Procedures for Developing Grounded Theory* (2nd ed.). Thousand Oaks: Sage Publications.

Sussman, N. M., & Tyson, D. H. (2000). Sex and Power: Gender Differences in Computer-Mediated Interactions. *Computers in Human Behavior, 16* (4), 381–394.

Suthers, D. D., & Hundhausen, C. (2003). An Empirical Study of the Effects of Representational Guidance on Collaborative Learning. *Journal of the Learning Sciences, 12* (2), 183–218.

Tidwell, L. C., & Walther, J. B. (2002). Computer-Mediated Communication Effects on Disclosure, Impressions, and Interpersonal Evaluations. *Human Communication Research, 28* (3), 317–348.

Turkle, S. (1995). *Life on the Screen: Identity in the Age of the Internet.* New York: Touchstone.

Turner, B. A. (1981). Some Practical Aspects of Qualitative Data Analysis: One Way of Organising the Cognitive Processes Associated with the Generation of Grounded Theory. *Quality and Quantity, 15* (3), 225–247.

van Bruggen, J. M., & Kirschner, P. A. (2003). Designing External Representations to Support Solving Wicked Problems. In J. Andriessen, M. Baker & D. Suthers (Eds.), *Arguing to Learn: Confronting Cognitions in Computer-Supported Collaborative Learning Environments* (pp. 177–204). Dordrecht: Kluwer Academic Publishers.

Veerman, A. (2003). Constructive Discussions through Electronic Dialog. In J. Andriessen, M. Baker & D. Suthers (Eds.), *Arguing to Learn: Confronting Cognitions in Computer-Supported Collaborative Learning Environments* (pp. 117–143). Dordrecht: Kluwer Academic Publishers.

Wallace, P. (1999). *The Psychology of the Internet.* New York, NY: Cambridge University Press.

Walther, J. B. (1992). Interpersonal Effects in Computer-Mediated Interaction: A Relational Perspective. *Communication Research, 19* (1), 52–91.

Walther, J. B. (1996). Computer-Mediated Communication: Impersonal, Interpersonal, and Hyperpersonal Interaction. *Communication Research, 23* (1), 3–44.

Walther, J. B., & Anderson, J. F. (1994). Interpersonal Effects in Computer-Mediated Interaction: A Meta-Analysis of Social and Antisocial Communication. *Communication Research, 21* (4), 460–488.

Wang, X., & Hurst, R. (1997). An Empirical Study of Computer-Assisted Class Discussion: Effects on Social Interaction and Group Dynamics. In *Proceedings of the Third International Conference on Foreign Language Education and Technology* (pp. 431–448). Victoria, Canada: University of Victoria Language Centre.

Warschauer, M. (1997). Computer-Mediated Collaborative Learning: Theory and Practice. *Modern Language Journal, 81* (3), 470–481.

Warschauer, M. (1999). *Electronic Literacies: Language, Culture, and Power in Online Education.* Mahwah, NJ: Lawrence Erlbaum Associates.

Webb, N. M. (1991). Task-Related Verbal Interaction and Mathematics Learning in Small Groups. *Journal for Research in Mathematics Education, 22* (5), 366–389.

Webster, M., & Driskell, J. E. (1983). Beauty as Status. *American Journal of Sociology, 89* (1), 140–165.

Weisband, S. (1992). Group Discussion And First Advocacy Effects In Computer-Mediated And Face-To-Face Decision Making Groups. *Organizational Behavior and Human Decision Processes, 53* (3), 352–380.

Weisband, S., & Kiesler, S. (1996). Self Disclosure on Computer Forms: Meta-Analysis and Implications. In *Proceedings of Human Factors in Computing Systems (CHI) 1996* (pp. 3–10). Vancouver, Canada: ACM Press.

Wenger, E. (1998). *Communities of Practice : Learning, Meaning, and Identity.* New York, NY: Cambridge University Press.

Wennerstrom, A., & Siegel, A. F. (2003). Keeping the Floor in Multiparty Conversations: Intonation, Syntax, and Pause. *Discourse Processes, 36* (2), 77–107.

Werry, C. C. (1996). Linguistic and Interactional Features of Internet Relay Chat. In S. C. Herring (Ed.), *Computer-Mediated Communication: Linguistic, Social and Cross-Cultural Perspectives* (pp. 47–63). Philadelphia, PA: John Benjamins Publishing Co.

Wright, J. C., Giammarino, M., & Parad, H. W. (1986). Social Status in Small Groups: Individual-Group Similarity and the Social "Misfit." *Journal of Personality and Social Psychology, 50* (3), 523–536.

Yates, S. J. (1996). Oral and Written Linguistic Aspects of Computer Conferencing. In S. C. Herring (Ed.), *Computer-Mediated Communication: Linguistic, Social and Cross-Cultural Perspectives* (pp. 29–46). Philadelphia, PA: John Benjamins Publishing Co.

Yin, R. K. (2003). *Case Study Research: Design and Methods* (Third ed.). Thousand Oaks, CA: Sage Publications.

Zajonc, R. B. (1965). Social Facilitation. *Science, 149* (3681), 269–274.

INDEX

Blocking, 57, 77–80, 84, 137, 138

Chat
Behavior in chat environments,
see disinhibition
Effect on quality, 120, 123–125
Effect on time on task, 125–129
History of chat, 12, 13
Linguistics, 13, 14, 126, 127,
138
Splitting attention in chat
environments, 127–129,
141, 142
Collaboration scripts, 31
Confidence, 17, 18, 72–76, 137
Conflict, role in learning, 28–31

Diffusion of responsibility, 57, 80,
81, 84, 136, 138
Discourse ethics, 32, 33
Disinhibition, 15, 16, 28, 31, 32,
45, 52, 136

Equality
In participation, 4, 7, 8, 104,
136–138
Sources of inequality, 19–22
Importance for learning, 18–20
Ethics education,
Goals, 89–92, 101, 102

Initiate-respond-evaluate (IRE)
cycle, 40–50, 78, 79

Internet Relay Chat (IRC), 12, 13

Language learning,
Challenges for adults, 23–25
Use of chat, 26–28, 68–71

Media effects on learning, 2, 3,
34, 35, 133, 134, 145–147
Motivation, 52, 53, 102, 103, 140,
141

Quality,
Measuring, 108–110
Defining, 86–89
Quasi-experimental methods,
105–119, 130, 131

Reflection, 70, 71

Self-awareness, 16–18, 56, 72–76,
83, 136, 137
Small group discussions, 92–95,
101, 102
Social cues, 56, 76, 77, 84, 133,
137
Social psychology,
Bystander effect, 53–57,
136, 137
Social facilitation, 17, 18,
72–76, 137
Social loafing, 52, 53, 140, 141
Social translucence, 141, 142
Synchronicity, 4, 142–145

Printed in the United States
205000BV00001B/4/A